TOM THOMPSON is from Belfast. in Harland & Wolff's Joiners' S nine years. He spent twenty-ei Authority as an Air Traffic Engi 1985 he set up the family busine of *Standing Room Only: Memories of Belfast Cinemas*.

# AULD HANDS

### The men who made Belfast's shipyards great

## TOM THOMPSON

·THE·
BLACK
·STAFF·
PRESS

First published in 2013 by Blackstaff Press
4c Heron Wharf
Sydenham Business Park
Belfast BT3 9LE

With the assistance of
The Arts Council of Northern Ireland

Typeset by CJWT Solutions, St Helens, England
Printed in Great Britain by the MPG Books Group

A CIP catalogue for this book is available from the British Library

ISBN 978 0 85640 911 0

www.blackstaffpress.com

*To that vast army of proud, industrious Islandmen
whose dedication and enterprise helped to create
the greatest shipyard in the world.
Their achievements and skills are
an inspiration to us all.*

# CONTENTS

## THE SHIPS

# INTRODUCTION

Queen's Island as it was in the 1950s remains vivid in my mind – the army of men toiling away (among them both the industrious and the skivers); forests of overhead cranes dominating the skyline; packed smelly tram cars; numerous milling bicycles; deafening noises from pneumatic tools; friendly or arrogant foremen; the threatening 'Hats'; the drama of seeing magnificent new vessels plunge into the Lagan for the first time; the gospel groups and gamblers; the accidents; and the shared moments of camaraderie, danger and fun.

Under the leadership of Harland, Wolff, Pirrie and others, an army of duncher-capped, dungareed workers, who thronged the Queens Road from 1858 onwards, transformed the industry into one which earned the epithet 'Shipbuilders to the World'. For the thousands employed there, 'the Yard' – sometimes jokingly referred to as the 'Boat Factory' – was never merely a work place. It became a way of life, a microcosm of the wider world outside. There were talented and conscientious workers, saints and scoundrels – all co-existing in a heavy industrial environment, building many of the finest ships in the world. Harry Fletcher, a shipwright who worked on Queen's Island for many years, recalled in his retirement that he didn't ever skip a day in case he missed anything – 'there was always something interesting going on'.

Apart from senior management, the majority of workers, although highly skilled, were drawn from the working class, and had only minimal educational qualifications. They were content in their positions and – despite the harsh, often dangerous conditions and the cranes, monster ships, hard work and incessant deafening noise – they were incredibly proud to be Islandmen, and spent their entire working lives in shipbuilding. The shipyards also produced, among others, a stream of writers, musicians, sportsmen and politicians (including an MP and a Belfast Lord Mayor) who made a significant impact both in Belfast and further afield.

In 1949, aged just sixteen, I began my career as an apprentice in the Joiners' Shop of Harland & Wolff. It was an almost inevitable step for me – my father worked as a plumber's helper in Harlands, my brother was a plumber and my grandfather had worked on the *Titanic*.

For the next nine years I was exposed to a culture of craftsmanship and dedication that was driven by motivation to achieve personal excellence in workmanship – a hallmark of most of the Queen's Island workforce. That legacy of striving for the highest quality work in those formative shipyard years has remained with me, particularly when doing woodwork. Even today, on regular visits to DIY stores, my trained eye easily detects warps, twists, shakes or any other defects in wood products. Anything purchased must meet my strict personal criteria.

I left Harland & Wolff in 1957 to pursue what at the time I felt was a more exciting career in the radio and television industry and, later, a twenty-eight-year-service with the Civil Aviation Authority as Air Trafffic Engineer. But like many former Island employees, I still retain a strong attachment to and fierce pride in the experience of building those fine ships that carried our workmanship and Belfast's reputation to every part of the world.

And while it is not possible to bring back that halcyon era when the Belfast shipyards touched the lives of so many people, I hope that the reminiscences in this book will revive happy memories for past shipyard men – or 'Auld Hands' as we often addressed each other – and alert a new generation to the workers' contribution to the historic local shipbuilding industry that placed our small province on the maritime map of the world. As a major part of our heritage of innovation and manufacturing, it should not be forgotten.

The English novelist L.P. Hartley wrote, 'The past is a foreign country: they do things differently there.' My time at Queen's Island is a 'country' I still choose to visit often, and inhabit again – with ever-increasing fascination, pride and affection.

# THE SHIPYARDS

# RESHAPING BELFAST

In 1791, William Ritchie, a successful Scottish shipbuilder, set up the first established shipbuilding industry in Belfast on the County Antrim side of the River Lagan. He had been attracted to Belfast by the planned improvements to the port by the Belfast Ballast Board (the forerunner to the Harbour Commissioners) who wanted to straighten the River Lagan and introduce more quays.

William Ritchie and his brother Hugh set up business at the Old Lime Kiln dock, just off today's Corporation Street. In 1800 they opened a dry dock (which, forty years later, would be known as Clarendon Graving dock) that could contain three 200-ton vessels at any one time. Today the dry dock, which is well-preserved, is the only tangible evidence of the legacy of the pioneer shipbuilder. Considerable credit is due to Ritchie for recognising the potential for shipbuilding on the Lagan site which was then, at least partially, blocked by slobland.

Other small shipbuilders soon followed Ritchie to the County Antrim shore – Ritchie & McLaine (later Charles Connell & Sons), Kirwan & McCune, Coates & Young and Alexander McLaine & Sons – though their constructions were mainly of modest tonnage, 50- to 200-tons.

During this time, the Ballast Board's plans to straighten and deepen the course of the River Lagan met with significant resistance from the Irish Parliament and it was only in 1839 that the prominent Dublin civil engineer, William Dargan, was contracted to begin work on the area.

The hundreds of acres of mudflats through which the shallow River Lagan meandered from Belfast Lough made direct navigation to the heart of Belfast impossible for large ships – at the Queen's Bridge the water level was only about two feet deep at high tide and cargo vessels had to transfer goods to smaller, low-draught ships at the Garmoyle Pool three miles downstream in order to deliver to the Belfast docksides. It was a serious impediment to the fast growing commercial and industrial life of the city. Dargan's solution was to make and dredge two new cuts into the slobland of the twisting channel, making the channel straighter and deeper.

Dargan's Channel was finished by 1841 and the spoil extracted from the slobland was enough to create an artificial island, Dargan's Island, on the County Down side of the river. In 1849 this was renamed Queen's Island in honour of Queen Victoria's visit to Belfast, and was known for a long time as a 'people's park' – a popular place of entertainment for Belfast citizens, complete with a large botanical greenhouse, a zoo and numerous bathing boxes.

By 1849 a second cut, the Victoria Channel, was complete, making direct navigation through the port possible. This resulted in the construction of modern dockside facilities which, in turn, attracted many new businesses – including the two main contributors to Belfast shipbuilding, Harland & Wolff and Workman Clark.

# HARLAND & WOLFF

In 1853, Robert Hickson, the new owner of Belfast Iron Works – an iron foundry in east Belfast that was making the move into shipbuilding – obtained a twenty-one-year lease on a site on the eastern bank of Queen's Island.

Hickson had strong business contacts in Britain and his new shipyard soon received its first contract – a wooden sailing ship commissioned by a company in Liverpool. More orders followed. However Hickson wasn't happy with the quality of work coming from his yard. He felt that his employees were lazy and that their work was sloppy, and in 1854 he fired his yard manager John Jordan. The nationally advertised vacancy caught the eye of Edward Harland – a former premium apprentice with Robert Stephenson in Newcastle on Tyne – and he was accepted for the position. Premium apprentices differed from ordinary trade apprentices – who earned a weekly wage of about six shillings (30p) a week – in that the former were usually from wealthy families who would pay around 100 guineas (£105) for their son to gain technical skills and eventually graduate into junior management positions.

Harland was a strict disciplinarian who did not crave popularity, and under his supervision the yard's output vastly improved. He had brought with him extensive shipping contacts – particularly with the English company, Bibby – and had poached three important orders from Bibby's usual builders, a shipyard on the Clyde. This was the beginning of a profitable relationship between Belfast and Bibby's. These orders also introduced the company to the larger shipping world and established it as a shipyard that could be depended on for reliability and innovation in ship design.

In 1858, when Hickson became financially overstretched and the company faced closure, Harland borrowed money from a relative and bought the troubled shipyard for £5,000. Three years later, German-born Gustav Wolff – who had been taken on as Harland's assistant in 1857 – became a partner in the company, and Harland & Wolff was formed.

Over the years the company would establish many lasting business connections, but the relationship with the White Star Line and its chairman, Thomas Ismay, would arguably prove to be the most important. In 1868 Ismay had bought the White Star Line, which was facing bankruptcy, for the token fee of £1,000, and the following year – with funding from Gustav Wolff's uncle, the prominent Liverpool merchant Gustav Schwabe – merged it into his new shipping consortium, the Ocean Steam Navigation Company (OSNC). As part of the contract with Schwabe, Ismay agreed to have his ships built by Harland & Wolff – it was the start of a long-lasting and profitable partnership.

As Harland & Wolff's reputation grew, so too did the yard. Further land was acquired from the people's park on Queen's Island for additional slipways and workshops, while the mudflats to the east of the park were also being reclaimed to link up with the County Down foreshore. In 1878 Harland & Wolff bought over the smaller shipyard of Alexander McLaine & Sons, one of their neighbouring competitors. Harlands now employed over one thousand men.

One of the key employees at this time was William Pirrie, an enterprising County Down man who had been a premium apprentice with the shipyard from 1862. He had progressed quickly through the management system and in 1874 became a partner in the firm. He was an ambitious individual and he became a driving force behind the aggressive expansion of the company. In his travels around Britain and Europe he

6

witnessed new ideas in ship design and fit outs and he brought the best of these to Queen's Island shipbuilding. Thanks to his initiative and vision for innovation and excellence, he managed to raise the profile of Belfast shipbuilding across the world. In 1895, following the death of Sir Edward Harland, Pirrie became the chairman of the company. It was a position he would hold until his death in 1924.

The status and construction capacity of Harlands was demonstrated in 1901 with the launch of the liner, *Celtic*, which at 20,904 tons was the largest in the world. This vessel consolidated the Yard's growing reputation as a major shipbuilder.

Pirrie then used his influence to convince Bruce Ismay, Thomas Ismay's son and successor, to place orders for three enormous passenger liners for the White Star Line. Opulent and luxurious, the *Olympic*, *Titanic* and *Britannic* would be of 'Olympic Class' – 46,000 tons each. They would be the largest passenger liners in the world, challenging the ships of other shipping companies for size and luxury.

During this time, Pirrie had also been expanding Harlands, acquiring yards in Liverpool, Clydeside, London and Southampton. Even with the tragic sinking of the *Titanic* in 1912, the firm thrived – leading the world not only in ships but in marine engines. By 1914, Harlands and Workman Clark accounted for one eighth of the world's total shipbuilding output, employing around twenty thousand men between them. The outbreak of war later that year was a boost to naval and merchant shipbuilding – more shipping was being lost to enemy action than could be replaced. Harlands made an outstanding contribution to the war effort, building or repairing over 400,000 tons while its rival yard, Workman Clark achieved 260,000 tons. At one time Harlands in its various operations employed around sixty thousand people.

7

In the early 1930s, in the wake of the Wall Street Crash and resulting recession, there was a worldwide slump in demand for shipbuilding. Both Workman Clark and Harland & Wolff were badly affected. With no orders, hundreds of workers were laid off, while on Queen's Island grass began to grow on the empty slipways. In a desperate attempt to stay solvent, Workman Clark made a tentative approach to Harlands about a merger, but the Harland yard was itself fighting off bankruptcy. Workman Clark struggled for on for a few more years, mainly on ship repair work, but was forced to close in 1935.

The former Workman Clark assets on the County Down side of the Lagan, including the 'Wee' Victoria Yard slipways and other facilities, were bought by Harlands who, thanks to preparations for the Second World War, had entered a new period of intense activity and profitability which would last for almost twenty years.

The onset of war meant a massive upsurge in the company's productivity, and the shipyard built or repaired a wide range of naval vessels, including corvettes, minesweepers and aircraft carriers. In the region of 10,000 field guns, 550 tanks and various other war armaments were also produced. At the beginning of the Second World War the British government had also asked Harlands to design and build the prototype for a new heavy tank. The 43-ton tank, the A22, which was named the *Churchill*, went into service in 1941 and subsequently fought in many theatres of war. With various modifications it emerged as the most successful British tank of the Second World War. With such an immense contribution to the war effort, the Queen's Island and the Short & Harland aircraft complex could not escape the attention of the German Luftwaffe for ever and they suffered loss of life and significant damage during the Belfast Blitz,

7 April 1941. That night an oil-filled parachute mine intended for the Shorts aircraft factory missed its target and drifted across the Musgrave Channel. Fire-watchers – whose role was to look out for and extinguish incendiary bombs – mistook it for a German parachutist, and rushed towards it. The mine landed on the roof of the Joiners' Shop (which was being used to assemble Stirling bombers) exploded and set the wooden tar-felt roof on fire. Four fire-watchers were killed instantly and the building, along with the much-needed aircraft that it contained, suffered extensive damage in the spreading inferno. Fifty aircraft were lost, while ships under construction on the slipways were badly damaged. Just over a week later, on Easter Tuesday (15 April 1941), several bombs hit Harlands' power station, as well as three vessels nearing completion. Other important shipbuilding facilities – including the electrical shop, machine tools and stores – were devastated under the air raids of that night which destroyed almost two-thirds of the yard's shipbuilding capacity.

It was over six months before production returned to normal levels, but Harlands rebuilt the damaged areas, and continued production until the end of the war when the company reverted to normal shipbuilding activities. At this time, Harlands were still using riveting as the chief method to build steel structures, even though welding had already been proven (by shipyards in the USA and elsewhere) to be a less expensive, more efficient method in building ships. Riveting was an antiquated process, but there was little incentive for management to change their practices since order books were full and handsome profits were being achieved. But tumultuous times lay ahead.

The 1960s saw a steep decline in traditional shipbuilding orders, and many UK shipyards faced closure. Upgraded facilities, nationalisation or bankruptcy were the only options. Harland & Wolff, still under local management, enjoyed a large degree of autonomy outside the UK nationalised shipyards, but was heavily subsidised by the British government. Some of this money was used to finance the modernisation of the Yard – the most significant outcomes of which were the construction of two enormous new cranes, Samson and Goliath, and a massive redesign of the shipyard.

As the new generation in shipping construction tended towards oil tankers and specialised marine structures, the yard's existing facilities and slipways were deemed inadequate and unable to utilise the new cranes' full potential. Further imaginative, but costly, changes were necessary.

A sixteen-million-pound dual-purpose building dock was constructed on the Musgrave Channel, formerly used for repair work, or as a fitting-out berthing for newly launched vessels. After sealing one end, the massive task of draining and excavating the channel began. (It is interesting to speculate about what the draining process revealed after workers had spent decades dumping materials overboard, either accidentally or intentionally!) This was followed by major reconstruction.

When completed, the building dock, straddled by Samson and Goliath, measured 1,834 feet long, 307 feet wide and 30 feet deep. It was the largest dock of its kind in the world, and proved that Queen's Island had the capacity to regain its former pre-eminence in shipbuilding. Vessels of up to one million tons could be built under dry-land conditions and then floated out from the flooded dock upon completion. Massive prefabricated sections of ship hulls, weighing up to 700 tons, could be built elsewhere in the shipyard then lifted into position in the dock. The radical modernisation programme also included the building of immense paint-house and fabrication facilities to support the building dock. The new facilities considerably reduced traditional construction time.

By the mid-1970s, Harland & Wolff was poised to exploit its state-of-the-art facilities in the emerging global ship-building market. But the anticipated influx of new orders to sustain the revamped shipyard did not materialise. Harlands had expected orders for 500,000-ton and 1,000,000-ton ships, but these never came. Aggressive pricing by competitors in Eastern Europe and Asia was relentlessly killing the viability of British shipyards. Harlands, under its shipbuilding-only remit, would not survive, and even management restructuring and diversification into non-ship construction could only slow a continuing decline in profitable activity.

In 1975, after regular mounting financial losses, the British government intervened and acquired all the company shares, although Harlands' status as a recipient of government funding meant that the Yard was not nationalised.

In 1989, Harland & Wolff was sold off in a management/ employee buyout in partnership with Fred Olsen, the Norwegian shipping magnate. With an investment of twelve million pounds, he became the main shareholder – few employee shares were taken up due to their high offer price, and these reverted eventually to Olsen. By this time, the number of people employed by the company had fallen to around three thousand.

For the next few years, Harland & Wolff specialised in building oil tankers and vessels for the offshore oil and gas industry. The last ship the company produced was the *Anvil Point*, a roll-on, roll-off ferry, in 2003. At 45,270 tons, this ship marked the demise of 144 years of shipbuilding in Belfast.

Then in October 2007 Goliath, which had been inactive for over five years, was re-commissioned for valuable metal engineering projects – including the construction of a series of bridges in Britain and Ireland, such as the Foyle Bridge in Derry/Londonderry and the restoration of Dublin's Ha'penny Bridge. The Musgrave dock continues to survive mainly on ship repairs, and offshore wind turbine and tidal power construction.

In the meantime, Olsen's new company, now called Harland & Wolff Holdings Plc, had redeveloped the vast, vacant shipyard site. Buildings were demolished, and most of Queen's Island, 185 acres to the west of the Musgrave dock, became a wasteland. Land that had been occupied by the former Harland & Wolff was sold to other property developers, and leased tracts of land were sold off for commercial development. Within a few years, almost all traces of this once-great shipyard had been erased.

Instead of Queen's Island, we now have the 'Titanic Quarter' – an area of luxury apartments, high-tech offices and warehouses. It is also home to the multimillion-pound *Titanic* attraction which has been set among surviving historic landmarks – including the huge Thompson Graving Dock (known today as 'The Titanic Dry Dock' – a term never used by shipyard men); the adjacent Alexander Graving dock (which was also shared with Workman Clark); the pump house; and the steamship *Nomadic*, the last surviving White Star Line vessel. But perhaps the most iconic and striking reminder of Harland & Wolff, once the greatest shipyard in the world, are Samson and Goliath – the two enormous yellow cranes that dominate the Belfast skyline.

# SAMSON & GOLIATH

For the first half of the twentieth century, the massive gantries in the Main Yard of Harland & Wolff were the last thing that emigrants saw as they left Belfast and the first sight to welcome home returning natives.

The Arrol gantries had been erected in 1909 to facilitate construction of RMS *Titanic* and her sister ships, *Olympic* and *Britannic*, but in the drastically changed economic market of the 1960s, they had become mostly redundant and so were dismantled and sold to a Belfast scrap dealer.

In their place, and thanks to a generous loan from the British government, Harland & Wolff had commissioned the erection of Samson and Goliath, two huge, biblically named cranes that were integral to the firm's modernisation strategy. The company was striving to meet a growing global market in new generation shipping and the two new cranes were major, speculative investments for an expected upsurge in demand. At the same time, their construction was also a defiant commercial and political gesture designed to signal that, despite the escalating Troubles, Northern Ireland remained an attractive location for potential investors.

Ironically, it was German company Krupps – the main armaments provider for Germany during the Second World War, whose products in the hands of the Luftwaffe had rained such devastating destruction on Queen's Island during the 1941 Blitz – who built the cranes. Goliath, at 315 feet high, was completed in 1969, while Samson, which is 30 feet taller, followed in 1974. With the ability to move along and above the dock, each crane has the lifting capacity of 840 tons.
If public access to the cranes was permitted, it would be the

ultimate white-knuckle experience in Ireland. But apart from qualified employees, and the occasional filmmaker or TV crew, few have had the opportunity. I have spoken to several people who have been lucky enough to see inside one of the cranes, and each described it as an unforgettable experience. The crane is accessed via a ground level entrance situated between the wheels of the enormous driving bogies which propel the entire structure along the building dock. Standing at the base you are struck by the sheer size of the leg, which seems to tower into space. It creates an overpowering sensation of awe – the engineering challenge of hoisting and positioning the 100-ton plus cantilever cross-gantry, including its cranes, on top of the 300-foot high vertical legs is mind-boggling.

Inside the main leg is a steel staircase, which only the supremely fit would use, and a lift that, with a series of loud and somewhat alarming noises, slowly makes its way to the summit, some 300 feet above ground. When the lift opens, it takes you directly into the control room where you are greeted by the huge diesel engine generator which produces a deafening level of noise and causes the entire structure to vibrate. Most of the crane's functions, including driving the complete structure along the ground, are controlled from that area.

In the control room there is also a crew rest room and kitchen, and a steel stairway which opens out onto one of the twin linking gantries that carry the mobile heavy-lift crane. One friend of mine described how he walked through the exit into the open air and had a moment of heart-stopping panic – the ground seemed alarmingly far below while the sky stretched infinitely above. Combined with this was the stiff wind that whipped around him as he ventured nervously onto the gantry, despite there being no more than a gentle breeze blowing when he was on the ground.

Few make their way across the gantry, but he gripped the safety rail that was fitted along the walkway (which gives access to the mobile crane and the far leg) and ventured out. He was rewarded with the most exhilarating sight – in the distance, the Mourne Mountains, Strangford Lough, Scrabo Tower and other well-known tourist landmarks were easily identified, while spread out below was Queen's Island, the harbour area and the city of Belfast. Familiar buildings and streets took on a new character and fascination. Toy-like vehicles and insect-sized people wound their way along the highways, oblivious to the watchers in the sky above them. Even more startling were the aircraft going to and from Belfast City Airport. Normally arriving and departing aeroplanes are viewed from ground level: on Samson or Goliath, the spectator is looking down at them. Duty crews who work on the cranes daily treat their hazardous environment with nonchalance. During my friend's visit he witnessed a man taking his lunch break at the edge of a gantry, legs swinging in space, while he enjoyed the fresh air and sandwiches, oblivious to, or unconcerned about, the danger of falling or being blown off by a gust of wind into the dock, 300 feet below. Perhaps this worker's apparent nonchalance comes from the fact that, despite the obvious dangers of working at extreme heights, there have been no fatal accidents during or since the cranes' construction. Though there have been some narrow escapes: when the H&W logo was being painted on Goliath's cross gantry, two painters were working from a cradle suspended from the upper crane. A sudden gust of wind billowed into one man's overalls, lifting him bodily out of the cradle. Quick action from his workmate, who grabbed him in time, prevented the painter from falling to his death in the dock far below.

There have been some narrow escapes for the cranes too. In November 1972, the IRA placed a bomb at Samson's base, intending to topple it. The bomb exploded but the crane, thanks to its sturdy construction, sustained only damage to its paintwork and experienced only minor interruption to its daily routine. Another bomb placed at Harland & Wolff's main offices that same day did more serious damage with loss of some company records.

On 17 April 2007, a 95-ton, 85-foot high, unattended dockside tower crane was left with its jib extended directly in the path of the slow-moving Samson. Witnesses to the impending crash could only stand horrified as Samson, with its warning klaxons screaming, bore down on the smaller crane unable to stop in time. In the impact the tower crane was completely demolished, flying remnants of steel girders struck an adjacent crane, and three painters narrowly escaped serious injury. No damage was caused to Samson. Harlands did not publicise the incident but a week later a workman's video of the crash was posted on YouTube. The Yard's response was guarded – a spokesman stated that the video 'appeared to be genuine' and that an investigation would be carried out but, to date, the inquiry's findings have yet to be released.

The two cranes have also faced threats of a more bureaucratic nature – in 2003 there was concern that they would have to be demolished due to a lack of suitable new orders, but the Northern Ireland Office minister at the time, Angela Smith, scheduled them as historic monuments. In listing them she stated, 'These cranes are an essential part of our city, our roots and our culture.'

Just like the Arrol gantries that preceded them, Samson and Goliath dominate not only the River Lagan area, but much of Belfast and today are the city's most prominent and recognisable feature, serving the city both practically and emotionally. Many cities have iconic landmarks – London has Big Ben; Paris, the Eiffel Tower. Belfast is proud to have Samson and Goliath, two of the world's largest travelling cranes.

# WORKMAN CLARK & COMPANY
# (THE WEE YARD)

'Workman, Clark & Company Ltd, Shipbuilders and Engineers, Belfast, Ireland', to give the firm its full title, was a major player in the British shipbuilding industry, though it often found itself overshadowed by Harland & Wolff, which had a higher profile. With the decline of British shipbuilding in recent years, the memory of Workman Clark has faded further into the mists of time and has become known by the sad epithet 'The Forgotten Shipyard'.

Frank Workman, born 16 February 1856, was a Belfast youth of Scottish stock. He was educated at Royal Belfast Academical Institution (Inst) and joined Harland & Wolff as a premium apprentice. Young Workman's time at Queen's Island was profitable. During his six years there he acquired knowledge of the technology and the commercial management skills needed to run a shipyard, and in 1879 (aged just twenty-three) he left Harlands to open his own company on the opposite side of the Lagan. His shipyard, known to locals as 'The Wee Yard', sat directly opposite Harlands on four acres of reclaimed land leased from the Harbour Commissioners. His defection and his choice of location for the new company were considered actions of extreme effrontery towards the employer who had trained him, but worse was to come. Soon after, Workman poached another key figure from Harlands, William Campbell, and installed him as yard manager, and in 1880 Edinburgh-born George Smith Clark – who had been an apprentice with Workman at Harlands – also defected to join the new shipyard. The loss of three valuable staff to a competitor right on their doorstep caused deep resentment in the Harland & Wolff management. But today, the young Workman team, confident and visionary, would be regarded as entrepreneurs, daring to break into an industry of which they had no serious corporate experience.

Clark's relatives put up part of the capital required to establish the new shipyard and the company was officially incorporated in 1880, when 150 workers were recruited and the first orders received. The yard's first ships, the *Ethel*, of 265 tons, and the *William Hinde*, 346 tons, were modest but respectable vessels for a new and unproven shipbuilder. In those early days, the company built hulls and coasters, but by 1881, Workman managed to secure an order for another ship, this time an iron screw four-masted barque from his in-laws, the Smith family of Glasgow who ran City Line. This led to a series of orders for sister ships which kept the company going until the 1870s.

By the 1890s the company was able to expand. The demand for longer and heavier ships of up to 5,000 tons, required greater building capacity, so in 1891 a further ten acres of land were leased from the Harbour Commissioners. At the same time Workmans began construction of Victoria Engine Works, an engine and boiler works, which meant it would no longer have to buy in the ships' engines and ancillary machinery. In 1893 it bought the bankrupted McIlwaine & McColl shipbuilding facilities on the east side of the Lagan, right on Harlands' doorstep! With ten slipways and forty acres, Workmans was poised to accept orders for larger ships, of up to 700-foot long and of various designs.

Belfast's latest shipyard quickly emerged as a major player in shipping circles in the British Isles. During its first year of operation Workmans had built a total tonnage that was only 7 per cent of Harlands' construction (which must have been reassuring to the larger shipyard); but by 1894, with a growing global reputation and an expanding list of shipowner clients, the Wee Yard's tonnage had risen to 50 per cent of Harlands', and was still growing. That year Workman Clark was listed fourth in the British shipbuilders register.

By 1902 Workmans had in place an impressive support infrastructure, state-of-the-art technology, including lifting equipment, and an enthusiastic design team. The company now employed over five thousand workers with the wide range of skills necessary to build and fit out a complete vessel on site – steelworkers (known as the black squads), joiners, upholsterers, painters and men with a broad gamut of other trades.

By this time, the demand for ships that were suitable for both passenger and cargo service was greater than the demand for basic cargo ships. Recognising this change in the trade, Workmans began to produce large steel screw steamers for this purpose. They also introduced (and built) the first turbine engine which was fitted in the liner *The Victorian*, and pioneered the design of refrigerated vessels that could transport meat, fruit and other perishables all over the world, thereby making cheaper food available to the British market.

As a result of these innovations, the total tonnage built by the Wee Yard surpassed that of Harland & Wolff in 1909, 1910 and 1911. This may have been a source of concern for Harlands, but in reality the two yards were complementary rather than competitive as each served different markets and shipping owners. Harlands specialised in large luxury liners but these were only a small part of Workmans' programme – it had a more diverse order book.

The outbreak of the First World War, however, brought major changes to both Belfast yards. Admiralty orders for various types of naval vessels had an important impact on the shipbuilding programmes, and Workmans had a significant share of naval construction. Between 1914 and 1918, seventy-seven ships, including cargos, were built. Another 1,396 were repaired or refitted, among them, dreadnoughts or capital battleships like HMS *Revenge*, and battle cruisers like HMS *Invincible*.

A little known aspect of the Yard's contribution to the war effort was the construction of specially designed vessels. Ostensibly conventional cargo ships, they were adapted as Mystery Ships, or Q-Ships, which, posing as unarmed merchant vessels, would lure German U-boats to approach. When the submarine was within range it would come under attack from the cargo ship's concealed guns. It was a dangerous tactic and often rebounded on the decoys with fatal results.

Other Workmans' ships incurred damage, or were lost altogether, during the First World War. On 21 January 1918 the SS *Teelin Head*, a cargo vessel which had worked for many years on the Baltic routes, was returning from France when it was attacked without warning by the German submarine UC–31 in the English Channel. The *Teelin Head* had been commissioned by the Ulster Steamship Company, owned by Gustav Heyn, and was built in 1883. At 1,718 tons, it was the first steel ship made by Workmans, and it also held significance for my own family. When the ship sank, all thirteen members of her Ulster crew perished, one of whom was my grandfather, James Marshall, an engineer. This loss compounded an earlier one as Marshall's son, also called James, was killed in France only two months before.

Another ill-fated wartime casualty with a Workman connection was HMS *Hampshire*. After its Belfast refit it was dispatched to take part in the Battle of Jutland campaign.

Immediately after action in Jutland it left the UK carrying Lord Kitchener on a vital diplomatic mission to Russia. On 5 June 1916, it struck a mine off Orkney. Only twelve members of the crew survived, and 643 others, including Kitchener, were lost. The site is today a recognised war grave. The death of Kitchener, a war hero, was a devastating setback for Britain at a critical point in the war.

By war's end Workmans had expanded, and the shipyard now extended over a hundred acres with a workforce of twelve thousand. The Wee Yard had come a long way from its four-acre premises of 1880.

In June 1918, the company set a world record, confirmed by the Lloyd's survey register, which has never been beaten. A riveter, John Moir, in a nine-hour working day, drove home 11,209 rivets. One can only speculate on the amount of sweat and protests that this must have drawn from the essential support team of fellow, lower-paid, workers – Heater Boys, Catch Boys and Holder Ons – who made the record possible. The Heater Boys' job was to heat the in-rivets to a critical temperature in his coke-fired brazier (the temperature was gauged by the colour of the rivet). He extracted the red-hot rivet from the fire with a set of tongs and threw it to the Catch Boy, who caught it in a special pair of asbestos mitts. The Catch Boy would then place the rivet in a tin before throwing it to the Holder On, who would hold the rivet in a pre-drilled hole in the steel plates to be joined in preparation for the riveter.

In June 1921, a review of Belfast industry ran in a special supplement in the *Belfast News Letter*. Among the companies reviewed was Workman Clark: 'This giant shipbuilding establishment has had a powerful influence on Ulster's industrial life and year-by-year it is going forward to still greater success. The company's works as they now stand are widely recognised as being among the most modern in the world ... the shipyard has worldwide fame and products of its skills are sailing the globe.'

Since 1880, Frank Workman and George Clark had retained firm control of their company and had steered it from being a minor shipyard – of which Britain had many others – to one with a world-class reputation that was comparable to that of Harland & Wolff. But by 1919 the founders were approaching retirement age, and decided to capitalise on the firm's success and considerable assets.

The Northumberland Shipping Company and its bankers negotiated a majority shareholding in the Belfast shipyard. Complete control eventually passed to the purchaser through a series of convoluted share transactions. A three-million-pound chunk of these was sold to a third party under the premise that the money would be used for Workman Clark expansion. In reality the money was diverted to a subsidiary of Northumberland to clear off their massive debts. Although the original owners retired wealthy, the financial security of the till then prosperous Belfast yard had been perilously weakened by the new owners' irregular manipulation of shares.

Post-war debts and a lack of cash to honour the shares issues, coinciding with a slump in shipbuilding worldwide, created a financial crisis which continued until 1928. By then the company had reduced its workforce by 75 per cent and had incurred a loss of three million pounds. Creditors and shareholders had lodged claims for fraudulent shares prospectuses and malpractice, and the reputations of Frank Workman, George Clark and the famous company they had founded were effectively destroyed by financial speculators and asset strippers.

In 1928 the company went into receivership and closed

temporarily, with all workers laid off until new owners could be found. Later that year, assisted by the Government Guarantee Act, the company reopened. Frank Workman had recently died and George Clark refused a request to return as a director on a restructured board. Under a new trading title, Workman, Clark (1928), there were still the formidable problems of low orders and the settlement of the debts incurred by the previous owners. Only when the shareholders and creditors who had been besieging the company agreed to a 33 per cent settlement, did the burden of debt begin to lift. Soon after, Workman, Clark received orders for two whaling factory ships of 17,000 tons each. These, together with repair work, kept the shipyard ticking over for another year.

Orders were scarce, and Workmans' usual customers had drifted off elsewhere, but prospects were encouraging for the new company and the yard was gradually making a recovery. However, the optimism was short-lived. On 29 October 1929 an economic and social catastrophe hit the world – the Wall Street Crash. Financial institutions and industries around the world were devastated, virtually overnight, and the two Belfast shipyards could not escape the fallout. Workmans was particularly exposed to a further downturn in shipping orders when shipping companies proved unable to invest in new tonnage.

Given its precarious financial situation, Workmans suggested a merger with Harland & Wolff. However they too had been hit by the Wall Street Crash and thousands of their workforce had been laid off. The acquisition of another ailing shipyard would not have helped their own survival prospects and they declined the merger.

Stripped of essential cash reserves due to earlier mismanagement, and unable to survive in a difficult economic climate, especially with the loss of confidence from the banks, the end was in sight for the newly restructured shipyard. By May 1932, after completion of *Erin*, a passenger/cargo ship, the board announced that all the slipways were empty and 90 per cent of the workers would be laid off.

Another unforeseen calamity involved the MV *Bermuda*, a 20,000-ton luxury liner built by Workman in 1927. It too was a victim of the world financial crisis and had been laid up in New York where it suffered disastrous fire damage. It was returned to Workmans for rebuilding but in May 1929, while still at the Belfast yard, another fire broke out and gutted the ship. The owner claimed negligence and demanded one million pounds of compensation from Workman Clark. As settlement, the shipyard, already stretched for cash to survive, bought the burnt-out shell and had it scrapped.

The shipyard struggled to survive. Despite receiving six significant orders for vessels of between 4,600 and 11,000 tons, and some repair work, by 1935 it was operating with a much-reduced workforce, and key staff were employed on a day-to-day basis. Many approaches to other shipbuilding interests, including the National Shipbuilders Syndicate, were unsuccessful. Too many British shipyards were in the same perilous situation.

On 20 April 1935, Workman Clark (1928) closed its gates for the last time. Perhaps if the company had managed to last a few extra years until 1939, the massive upsurge in wartime shipbuilding and the post-war shipping boom that rescued Harland & Wolff, would have saved Workmans too, but as it was, the company's considerable assets on both sides of the Lagan were put up for auction in September 1935. Their South Yard, also known as the Victoria Yard, with the Victoria Works and other east side facilities were purchased by Harland & Wolff. This was a shrewd transaction by their former rivals as one of Harlands' conditions of purchase was that the Harbour Commissioners would not permit future shipbuilding on Workman's old site on the other side of the Lagan. Obviously the past lesson of having a formidable rival shipbuilder on their doorstep had been well learned. There was, however, a temporary reprieve of this rule in the mid-1950s. A high prefabrication building was erected over several of the old slipways to enable Harlands to fulfill an Admiralty order for six minesweepers which could not be built on the fully occupied slipways on Queen's Island.

Various alternative uses were suggested for the abandoned shipyard site, including ship breaking, but nothing came of these suggestions, and when the land leases were auctioned off in 1939, most of the buildings were razed to the ground and the site cleared. It was a sad end to a company which, over fifty-five years, had made an important contribution to Ulster's economy and had provided many much-needed jobs.

Three years later, on 26 January 1942, an important use for the land was found, at least temporarily, when Workmans' Dufferin Dock was used as the landing point for Major-General Russell P. Hartle and the 34th Infantry Division, the first US division deployed to Europe during the Second World War. That day, over three thousand American troops landed in Belfast, though three hundred thousand would eventually pass through Ulster. Northern Ireland had become the vital launching pad for the eventual liberation of Europe from Hitler's armies.

Little evidence of the world-class Workman Clark shipyard remains, except for one poignant reminder: mounted on an external wall of the Thompson Pump House is a memorial to the 124 'officers and men of the Belfast Workman shipyard who fell in the Great War of 1914–1918'. The memorial was commissioned by Frank Workman, whose only son Edward, a former shipyard director, had died of wounds in France in January 1916. Designed and built by artist Sophia Rosamond Praeger, the memorial was unveiled by Sir Edward Carson on 8 August 1919 and it shows Edward Workman in profile, flanked by the names of the other men from the shipyard who died. The memorial, the wording on which is now hardly legible behind the plastic sheeting, was relocated from Workmans' premises when the company closed in 1935.

The Thompson Pump House and other isolated relics give little impression of the dynamic hub of Ulster industry that once flourished there. The former Workman site, sandwiched between the Dufferin Road and the River Lagan, is currently fenced off and used for storing coal. The Fitting Out Basin in Dufferin Dock, built in the shipyard's latter years, is today only an inlet into the main dock, with the wooden jetties long removed. The Milewater Fitting Out Basin was partially filled in for building ground. Belfast has all but forgotten Workman Clark.

In Australia, however, a pristine relic of The Wee Yard has survived. The *Polly Woodside* – an iron-hulled three-masted barque of 678 tons and one of three ships built for Belfast shipowner, W.J. Woodside – is now the main exhibit at the Melbourne Maritime Museum. Named after Woodside's wife (Marian 'Polly' Woodside), the vessel was launched in 1885 and travelled between British ports and South America, carrying nitrates and coal. In 1904 it was sold to a New Zealand company and renamed *Rona*. Its long seagoing career covered the Atlantic and Pacific routes, and it was even used for a time by the Australians during the Second World War.

The historical significance of the ship was recognised when it was purchased by the Australian National Trust in 1968. Since then a vast amount of time and money has been spent on restoring it to its original condition. In 1988 it was awarded the Maritime Heritage Award by the World Ship Trust – the first for a restored merchant ship – and in 2007, it was added to the Victorian Heritage Register.

Today the ship is berthed in a new multi-million dollar dock at the Melbourne Maritime Museum – which is now known unofficially as the *Polly Woodside* Museum. On its stern is a sign which simply reads, '*Polly Woodside*'.

The poet Crawford Howard – famous for his satirical shipyard poem 'The Diagonal Steam Trap' – told me some years ago of a visit he made to the museum. On a tour of the bridge of the *Polly Woodside*, he was greeted with a pleasant surprise – the ship's bell is inscribed, 'Workman Clark Ltd, Belfast'. Howard described how, on a sudden impulse, he flung his arms around the bell to give it a hug and a kiss, with the remark, 'You're a long way from home, old girl.'

# THE MEN

T

# THE APPRENTICE

It seemed inevitable that I would follow in my father's footsteps and work in the shipyards. A successful interview with Jimmy McGrath, head foreman joiner, six months before my sixteenth birthday, confirmed that path.

Shortly after my birthday, I presented myself at Harland & Wolff's main offices on the Queens Road where a rather serious official solemnly briefed me about company regulations and the responsibilities of an apprentice. I gave him my £5 deposit (hard-earned by my mother) and was given a copy of the firm's indentures for the five-year apprenticeship – no smoking on the premises, no strike actions, good attendance, obligatory evening classes, and other strict conditions which sounded more like rules for an army recruit than regulations for a job in industry.

At 7.30 a.m. on a cold and miserable January morning I joined my father on the long walk from our east Belfast home to the shipyard. In my new blue boiler overalls and carrying my first 'piece' – a lunchbox containing a double-ended canister of tea and sugar and a small milk container – I was excited to be entering this new world. But mixed with the excitement was a sense of anxiety. I recalled the stories about the hazards of shipyard life that my father had told me over the years – accidents, decapitations, mutilations, deaths and injuries from slipping crane loads, and fatal falls from great heights. One of my uncles, who was a joiner at the shipyard, had recently fallen to his death through an asbestos roof. It was difficult to escape the feeling that working on Queen's Island was akin to living in a war zone and that it would be difficult to survive unscathed.

My father and I parted company at the Musgrave Channel where he was working on a ship being fitted out after its launch, and I made my way to the vast Joiners' Shop on the Queens Road. Once inside, the immediate impact was of hundreds of workbenches that stretched away as far as the eye could see, each occupied by two workmen. Everyone was toiling away. Somewhere in the background, woodworking machinists contributed their own unique noisy decibels to the scene.

I was directed to assistant foreman Bobbie Moffatt (the Gaffer) who oversaw a section of about forty workers, but my initial enthusiasm soon faded when he told me, 'Thompson, there are no benches or mates available yet – until then you are on the gluepots.' For the first three weeks in the new job I stood all day by an electric boiler heating evil-smelling glue for the squad's joiners. It was an isolated, miserable task with few people to talk to, and was certainly not living up to my expectations – I was there to learn a trade! I thought about quitting and returning to my previous job as a milk delivery boy which, at thirty shillings a week, paid better than the frustrating shipyard one. But common sense (and my parents' persuasion) prevailed.

Eventually the glue-making ordeal ended and I was allocated a bench with a young and friendly journeyman mate, Bill from Glenavy. But here again, the work wasn't quite what I was expecting. My modest contribution to the job was daily, endless sandpapering, with strict instructions: 'Be more careful' or 'Don't rub against the grains. Faulty sanding will make the Gaffer reject the complete finished job.' For me the appeal of learning the joinery trade was fading fast – making glue and wasting time on a simple task like sandpapering was hardly a portent for more exciting times ahead. But I persevered and soon I began to get valuable experience.

My helpful mate constructed my first toolbox – it was 3 foot long, the ends dovetailed by a sympathetic machinist. An on-site painter gave it a coat of black paint, a piece of machine belt served as a handle, and a drawer lock was attached to complete a professional-looking toolbox as good as any others about. Making toolboxes for new apprentices was a common practice, but had to be done secretly, in case a foreman spotted the unofficial activity. It was a 'wink and nod' custom.

At that point I did not have any tools for the box, but it was multifunctional, and travelled with me around the Yard for years, serving as a seat at lunch breaks, a sawing stand or a work stool. It also served for a time as safe storage for my lunch materials. For over fifty years I treasured the box and its contents, which were still useful, until one day it was stolen from my business warehouse. It was an upsetting loss.

Gradually I was able to fill the box with tools, either by buying them new with my meagre weekly pay of twenty-four shillings (£1.22), or from auctions in the Joiners' Shop. But it was a while before my kit was complete and I often had to use my mate's extensive collection of tools. This would always be a delicate operation as tradesmen protected their personal tools with the vigilance usually reserved for guarding the crown jewels. Although tools were strewn around the bench, it was etiquette to request, 'Bill, can I borrow your tenon saw?' (or whatever item I needed at the time). The request was always granted, if sometimes with obvious reluctance, but it was certainly not the done thing to help yourself. It was a culture of obsessive possession that I would later embrace.

I learnt a lot from my friendly mate, Bill. One day, as I worked away at my side of the bench, I was startled to hear him exclaim, 'They've given us more of that bloody bastard mahogany!' Now, Bill was normally politely spoken and it was the first time I had heard him use coarse language. When he saw my reaction, he quickly explained the outburst: 'bastard mahogany' was the name widely used in the trade to describe a low-grade imported mahogany that was not desirable for quality workmanship. As a young apprentice I mischievously used the term outside the Yard (though without the 'bloody' prefix) to shock my friends, before explaining what the phrase meant. I then felt that I had impressed them, proving myself to be an erudite scholar of timber varieties.

In time, I grew more competent and Bill began to trust me with some of the more interesting bench work – cabinets, desks and other cabin furniture. I soon learned (albeit painfully) respect for the sharp-edged tools used on these items. I had heard horror stories of workers losing fingers and even eyes through carelessness with tools, and had thought that I was prepared, but I still managed to have my share of mishaps. Several times I found myself at the Main Yard first-aid post nursing cuts that needed several stitches. The attendant would apply these, none too gently, and I would be dispatched back to my bench with a brusque 'Don't think this will get you time off today. Away back to your work.' If sympathy was sought it was never forthcoming from anyone.

Along with knowledge of the trade, I was also fast-learning the ways of the Yard itself. A unique system of timekeeping was used in Harlands – each worker was issued with a 'Board', a slim 2 x 1 inch wooden object with an indent at one end on which would be stamped the employee's work number. The Board was the worker's identity card throughout his shipyard career, regardless of the area of Queen's Island in which he worked and was used to report in and out of work each day via a timekeeper's office. It was meant to be an effective method of recording actual attendance at work, but some wily workers found means of bypassing the system. They would get apprentices, or other younger workers, to hand in their board at the end of the day while they found a way to slip out early. It was a risk-free action, as hundreds of other unidentified hands were pitching their boards through the pigeonhole at the same time. In this way men were able to obtain official pay credits even when nowhere near the shipyard. This practice was common on the slipways and fitting out wharfs but was made more difficult in the yard's workshops by the tight discipline and ever-vigilant foremen.

The men in the workshops, however, had their own little cheats on regulations. There were no official tea breaks across the shipyard in the long morning or afternoon shifts – a situation long tolerated due to a fear of authority – but workers would smuggle in flasks of tea and consume them furtively whilst still working at the bench, keeping an anxious lookout for foremen. The same foremen could retire at any time to their warm offices for their own tea breaks. It was an unfair regulation that was only corrected many years later.

The need for a hot cup of tea after a hard morning's work was a strong one, and at 12.25 p.m., at the sound of the lunch break klaxon, there was a stampede of hundreds of workers to the outside troughs where rows of water taps provided boiling water. Many older joiners did not wish to join the melee of jostling workers in the scramble for hot water so apprentices would gather up their cans for them – usually Heinz beans cans with wire handles – and fill them at the taps. Each tea can earned the apprentice one shilling a week and the lucky ones could earn seven or eight shillings a week. The 'Tea Can Run' was a useful supplement to pocket money. Not being enterprising enough I never acquired more than two tea cans, but it was a significant addition to my normal five shillings pocket money.

Harlands had proven, to me at least, to be generous employers. Some of my colleagues felt that senior management had a ruthless and detached attitude towards its workers (though, arguably, this sort of attitude might be expected from any industrial monolith) but my experiences were different. One day, while at home recuperating from a hospital operation, I unexpectedly received a VIP pass to attend the launch of the SS *Southern Cross*. On another occasion, after a prolonged absence due to a more serious health problem, the company awarded me generous time credits towards my apprenticeship period. This meant they were paying me journeyman's wages before the full 'Improver' catch-up time was reached. Those unsolicited and generous gestures probably encouraged my perception of Harland & Wolff as benign, caring employers.

As I neared the end of my first year's apprenticeship, the future was bright. I was due a small pay rise and a transfer to one of the ships under construction on the slipways and, as one of the shipyard's recognised elite trades (along with the electricians), my boiler suit overalls had long been replaced with a joiner's white apron – a perceived, if not widely accepted, symbol of superiority. For a keen sixteen-year-old apprentice pushing seventeen, life in the shipyard was not too bad after all.

# THE AUCTION

Tommy Graham, a tall, sturdily built joiner, conspicuous at any time, was standing on a box in the middle of the Joiners' Shop. It was lunchtime and he was surrounded by a crowd of eager or merely curious tradesmen and apprentices. A complete set of woodworking tools was laid out neatly on a bench beside him. His assistant, an apprentice, was holding up a slim wooden tool for all to see. 'What am I bid for this fine rabbit plane?' said Graham. 'Try and buy it in Jamison & Green's and it'll cost you at least one pound, ten shillings. Who'll start off with two shillings? Two and six! Three shillings! Going! Going! Gone! At three and sixpence to that tall skinny apprentice with the clean apron!'

I was over the moon. I had obtained another item of woodworking equipment to place in my embarrassingly sparse toolbox. The 'rabbit' plane, or rebate plane, its correct name, was an essential tool for any aspiring tradesman, and I had obtained it at a bargain price.

Lunchtime auctions of former joiners' tools were a regular feature in the huge Joiners' Shop. It was a tradition that had grown over many years. When a tradesman died, a trade union official, or other elected figure would, after a respectful period, approach the widow and suggest that her husband's work tools could be auctioned off and the proceeds given to her to help to alleviate her new circumstances. Consent was almost always given as the tools were still on Harlands' premises.

News circulated by word of mouth around the Shop that an auction was taking place. To ensure efficiency and integrity, the auctions were always carried out by a trade union member or another respected figure. Tommy Graham, as a shop steward and works convenor, was well qualified to conduct an auction.

For a young apprentice such as myself, the auctions were the only consistent source of good quality tools at affordable prices. Full price woodworking tools from hardware suppliers were too expensive to purchase so early in our career. For example, in 1949, even with my first week's pay of twenty-four shillings and four pence (£1.22), and pocket money of five shillings a week, my parents still had to give me another four shillings so that I could buy a steel record smoothing plane from a dealer.

The auctions by their nature were sombre reminders of the passing of former workmates, but they also became sources of entertainment and were seldom without moments of humour. At one auction the bidding was painfully slow to take off. Graham, in his usual coarse, direct manner, and with patience running low, burst out, 'I didn't know there was so many bloody Ballymena men worked in the shipyard. Put your hands in your pockets, for God's sake. The moths won't ate you. Don't you know this is for Arthur's wee woman? Let me see your hands up with those bids.'

On another occasion, when even the apprentices were not showing their usual enthusiasm, and buying and bidding was lukewarm, Graham decided to inject more urgency and spice into the proceedings just as the lunch break was drawing to a close. From his pedestal, he lambasted the reluctant onlookers. 'You buggers are all standing there like you're waiting for the Second Coming. I bet if Marilyn Monroe was on this box selling off her clothes you would be batin' each other over the head to catch her eye and make a bid. In ten minutes you would have had every stitch off her back.' Though ludicrous, the image of Marilyn Monroe on a box in the Joiners' Shop trading her modesty for the highest bids was effective. Graham, by no stretch of the imagination a Marilyn Monroe look-a-like, had broken the mental log jam of reluctant buyers and brisk bidding began. The toolbox and its contents were sold off in record time. That evening the joiner's widow received a larger than usual cash payment for her husband's equipment. Little did she know that a famous actress had contributed to the welcome cash windfall.

Sadly, the day arrived when Tommy Graham's own tool kit was laid out for auction. Part of my apprenticeship was spent under his genial supervision and it had been a stress-free period, compared with other journeymen's experiences. He spent a lot of his time away from the bench as he was often called off to settle demarcation disputes between joiners and shipwrights. Shortly after I had been transferred to another location – a ship – I was shocked to learn that Tommy had collapsed and died at his bench. His final exit from the Joiners' Shop was a sad and distressing occasion for all his workmates. Two ambulance men were unable to remove him because of his large size. The delicate problem was only solved when four joiners used the door Tommy had just completed to convey the body to the ambulance. Undignified it may have appeared to some, but to others it was a fitting tribute and touching farewell to a woodworker and trade unionist who had dedicated most of his working life in service to Harland & Wolff and his fellow workers.

# THE JOINERS' SHOP

During my time in the vast five-acre Joiners' Shop, the most exposed section was supervised by Gaffer Frankie Anderson. This particular area was adjacent to a block of three glass-fronted offices that housed the Head Foreman (Jimmy McGrath), his assistant (Victor Johnston) and Anderson himself. For anyone prone to loafing, excessive chatting or doing 'homers' (private projects made with shipyard materials, usually during working hours) it was a stressful location to work in. But to some workers, such constraints only represented a challenge. Homers were still made; the forbidden tea breaks still occurred; the time allotted for trips to the toilets – which were supposed to be limited to seven minutes each morning and afternoon – were exceeded.

About five hundred men toiled under the same roof. Each section or squad contained around forty tradesmen and their apprentices, and about 75 per cent of the vast workplace was crowded with squads of joiners and their benches. The large central area was occupied by woodworking machinery – planers, dovetailers, circular saws, jigsaws, drills, and a range of other equipment – which generated a continuous cacophony of teeth-grinding and ear-shattering sounds. At one end of the Shop, several sample rooms and cabins had been set up as exhibits to show potential customers the quality of workmanship and style available. It was the men who really made the Joiners' Shop, though, and Frankie Anderson's squad had a wide range of shipyard characters.

In a remote corner of the Shop, Jimmie, the one-legged painter (a man who never refused to paint an apprentice's new toolbox), reigned supreme in his little one-man empire.

At a bench in my section sat Jock Spence and his young mate, Victor. Jock was a Scottish joiner and he peppered most of his conversations with verses from Robert Burns – who he had declared to be 'the best poet in the world'. Jock was also notoriously tight – if he was ever approached for a donation towards a charitable cause, his usual response would be 'I'm only a poor pensioner. Ye know ye canny take the breeks of a Heilan man.' Victor, meanwhile, wasn't considered a proper joiner since he was a 'townie', having served his time outside the Yard. Townie joiners were invariably referred to disdainfully as 'wood butchers', reflecting a prevalent shipyard sense of superiority.

Another strange character was Jimmy Quaill, from the Shankill Road. He had served in the First World War and few escaped hearing about his exploits. He also had the irritating habit of relating to one and all the story of a recent operation he had had for an eye problem. No details were spared. He often boasted that, by taking out his eye, he could look behind him without turning his head! He would offer to remove the eye and let fellow workers handle it but no one accepted – particularly during the lunch break. The reluctance always puzzled him.

A joiner called Jordan claimed he had seen active service on American aircraft carriers and would tell anyone who would listen about the wooden flight decks that these had, making them vulnerable to enemy air attack. 'British carriers,' he claimed, 'especially the Belfast-built ones, have a better reputation for sustaining heavy damage.' Billy Morrison from Killyleagh would remind everyone that the founder of the British Museum in London was Hans Sloane, a Killyleagh resident.

Nearly every worker in the Joiners' Shop had his own foibles and eccentricities, and I was no different. Over the years I developed a close friendship with Andy Carville, a joiner from the Old Lodge Road, with whom I shared interests: namely playing the accordion and constructing wireless sets (basic radios). My interest had started in my first year in the Yard and from simple crystal sets with headphones, I had progressed to more ambitious projects.

Every day, when Anderson was out of sight, Andy and I left our benches to go to the outside toilet block and lock ourselves in a cubicle together. We would spend the time chatting about accordions and radio. More 'traditional' topics, such as football or girls, were seldom, if ever, discussed. Occasionally we would be joined by another accordion and radio enthusiast, Billy Lonsdale (who we nicknamed 'oscilloscope', after a piece of test equipment). It was a tight squeeze in a cubicle with three people sitting on each others' knees, but these were much-anticipated respites from standing at a bench for hours at a time.

John, the toilet attendant, would regularly come round to bang cubicle doors and threaten to inform McGrath about anyone who was overstaying their official time of seven minutes. But he was a tolerant man and he never did.

Out of my friendship with Andy, a promising business idea developed. Andy often had engagements to play the accordion at parties and wedding functions. I had built an amplifier out of ex-wartime radio parts purchased in Smithfield Market and housed it in an attractive custom-built cabinet – another homer, courtesy of Harland & Wolff! It appeared logical to combine the two skills and use my equipment as a sound system to augment Andy's playing. The first functions were successful and profitable. I provided the equipment – the amplifier, a modified wind-up gramophone, speakers and records. Soon we received a booking to provide amplification for a major event at St Mary's Hall in Bank

Street in the city centre. During a dummy run, I connected the equipment as usual and switched it on ...

Later we had difficulty in recalling what came first – the frightening explosive bang, the ball of smoke from the amplifier or the lights in the hall flickering on and off. The engagement was scrapped. The cause was a simple one – the amplifier had been built to operate from a DC mains supply, and at that time the Belfast Corporation was converting the city centre supplies to AC – but the St Mary's Hall incident killed off our business enterprise, and Andy continued his music career without my unpredictable electronics.

# IODINE AND CO.

The men of the shipyards were fond of assigning nicknames to their fellow workers – possibly because, in an environment where there were thousands of workers, a nickname was easier to recall than a person's actual name. The most basic names often related to a worker's hometown. In the Joiners' Shop, most people were familiar with men called 'Annalong' or 'Killyleagh' without ever knowing their real names. Some nicknames were more inventive. In the Main Yard first-aid post, the attendant could be relied upon to dispense one particular remedy for almost every ailment or injury. According to him, and regardless of the circumstances, a liberal application of iodine was a panacea. It was widely believed the same treatment would be used to heal a broken leg. It was inevitable that he would acquire the nickname 'Iodine Willie'.

Iodine Willie's predecessor, who must have been trained at a different medical school, also had a favourite one-fix remedy when he worked in that post. His treatment was to use washing soda, then give the injured party strict instructions to continue the same procedure at home. 'Washing Soda', as he was invariably called, had a sideline in running a mini-shop on the first-aid premises, and would even handle the occasional bet for punters – the original 'One-Stop Shop'.

In most cases the nicknames chosen were harmless and humorous, if accurate. But they could occasionally be cruel, especially when referring to a mannerism or an aspect of a worker's appearance – Big Nose, Wing Ears, Horse Face, No Talk, Barking Dog, His Nibs and many more were familiar to their workmates. Shipwright Harry Fletcher, often referred to as 'Bungalow', was, allegedly, a workmate with nothing upstairs; 'Forty Watts' was not too bright; 'Big Hallion' and 'Wee Hallion' were useful men to have around when heavy lifts were required; 'Sammy One Arm', from the Shore Road, had been badly injured in an IRA bomb attack on his local pub. But despite his handicap he was a popular character around the Yard and a raconteur of entertaining stories.

In most cases the recipients of nicknames, including managers, were aware of their shipyard alter egos, and usually accepted them with good grace. A person's relative, however, could be a different story. Two neighbours were chatting one day, when one casually mentioned 'Budgie' Kerr, a none-too-popular foreman. The other person, who was Kerr's sister, was livid and a blazing row ensued between former close friends. Neither spoke to the other for years.

# DO AS I SAY ...

During my time at Harlands there was one particular Gaffer, Bertie Hamill, who really did not like apprentices. In fact, he did not like many people at all except his own cronies in the Joiners' Shop, and he had few real friends there. But apprentices in particular were the bane of his life (which he believed should be carefree) and he did not want the responsibility of overseeing and training youngsters who would prefer to skive, talk or smoke, than do a day's work. According to him the best place for apprentices was in the army to learn discipline and respect for authority. Every day he would share with close friends and fellow foremen the irritation he felt at the (apparent) lack of moral values shown by the apprentices, and most of the tradesmen under his supervision.

He was strongly opposed to the practice of doing homers, and anyone caught red-handed or even suspected was given a severe warning with the threat that a repeat would result in instant dismissal and criminal charges. As a result his squad enjoyed the lowest rate of homers in the shipyard.

Thanks to his tightly enforced regime there was none of the relaxed, pleasant ambience that other squads, with popular Gaffers, seemed to enjoy. For many apprentices, a daily visit to the dentist would carry less dread than facing Hamill's grim, unsmiling features.

Suddenly, to most workers' delight, he was replaced one day with a more amiable Gaffer and was never seen again in the Joiners' Shop. A shocking explanation soon emerged. He and a colleague had been running a shop-fitting business and the materials used by his accomplice to fit out public houses and other commercial premises had been stolen from the Joiners' Shop and other parts of the shipyard. It was a daring, hypocritical venture that earned Hamill and his accomplice a five-year sentence in prison.

Understandably, few of his former joiner colleagues expressed sympathy at his misfortune in being caught and the normal farewell collection for retiring staff did not take place.

# THE BOATS

One day in 1950, as I was approaching the end of my first year as an apprentice, a journeyman mate and I were constructing a wardroom charts table in the Joiners' Shop when we became aware of an approaching figure. Bobbie Moffatt, the Gaffer, wearing the traditional bowler hat and brown dust coat, was coming to my side of the bench. I was alarmed. Had I been observed snatching a surreptitious sip of tea from my hidden flask? Or worse, had the half-completed homer under the bench been spotted? To my relief, it was neither.

Moffatt, who had always displayed an endemic dislike of apprentices, barked out, 'Thompson, pack your toolbox tomorrow morning. Your first year is up and you're going to the boats. Report to Barney McMahon in the Abercorn Yard and remember – no messing about.' This was the news all apprentices looked forward to. The second and fourth years of our five-year training period were spent on ships under construction in various locations in the shipyard. By curious tradition, the steel monsters built in the shipyard were seldom referred to as 'ships': they were always known as boats. So to the men of the shipyards, the 38,000-ton HMS *Eagle* (then fitting out at the Deep Water Wharf) shared the same marine categorisation as the Lairds Hire rowing boats in Bangor Bay.

I looked forward to having a break from the strictly regimented Joiners' Shop and a Gaffer's vigilant supervision. In the gruelling nine-and-a-half-hour days spent in the Joiners' Shop, a forty-minute lunch break was the only respite, and any more than twice-daily visits to the toilets were viewed with suspicion. By all accounts, working on the boats was a vastly different experience: there was a more relaxed regime with less supervision, provided the work was completed satisfactorily and on time.

Next day, with trepidation, I sought out the foreman's office at the Abercorn Yard. It may have been a memorable milestone in my career but to Barney McMahon, interrupted during his tea break, I was just another greenhorn offloaded into his squad, taking up his tradesmen's valuable time with training. He had no welcome ceremony or pleasantries for me. Instead he said curtly, 'See those four boats on the slips? Go to number 1400 and report to Johnny Dennison, the Gaffer. He'll soon sort you out. I know too well you young buggers when you cut loose from the Joiners' Shop. You're here to work and not skive. Away you go.' It was hardly an auspicious introduction for a nervous seventeen-year-old to a strange, new workplace. I made my way out of the office, and to the slipways.

Around the yard's four slipways were ships under various stages of construction. Swarming around these were hundreds of trades plying their skills – steel workers (the Black Squads), plumbers, electricians and others. Overhead towered the cantilever cranes, their operators isolated in a cabin which was 150 feet above ground. With consummate skill and precision, and amidst chaotic activity on the decks, these operators lowered heavy loads of steel sections into designated positions. For me, the immediate impact was the noise. There was no escape. The din of continuous riveting could be heard on the Newtownards Road, a mile away, so the effect at close quarters was overwhelming, threatening to shatter the eardrums. Conversation was difficult, and was often only achieved by shouting directly into a colleague's ear.

Boat number 1400 was a 9,000-ton oil tanker propped up on dry land astride a slipway. On all sides it was cocooned in wooden staging festooned with numerous ladders, pipes and cables, all obscuring the massive steel hull. The Stagers – whose job it was to erect this temporary narrow wooden structure for other trades to work on – were strong, fearless men. Their job, I always felt, was one of the most dangerous in the yard.

On the narrow staging, over 100 feet from the ground, workmen with heavy equipment toiled, only inches away from falling to their death or sustaining serious injury. The tanker was still mainly a steel shell with only bare interior decks installed – a marked contrast to the enclosed comfortable environment of the Joiners' Shop I had just left on that cold, dismal January morning. But Johnny Dennison, my new Gaffer, was a friendly, approachable person, who always had time to chat about non-work topics, even with apprentices – most other Gaffers did not permit such interaction. Dennison was devoid of the formalities of his grade – no bowler hat or dust coat as worn by indoor foremen. On the boats only senior management (known as 'Hats') sported the trappings of authority. When they appeared aboard a ship, an effective grapevine system would alert everyone, 'There's a hat about, look busy!' Or, 'Don't be caught making tea at the Heater Boy's fire.'

Working conditions aboard 1400 were primitive. Below decks, with doors and portholes yet to be fitted, there was no protection against the wintry elements. At times snow had to be cleared from indoors to allow work to progress. Workmen toiled and had their lunch breaks in the most squalid conditions. In the evenings, the ships became a scavenging ground for rats hunting for food scraps left from lunchtime. There were also no toilets aboard the ships – they were located at the bottom of the gangway. As a result, workers would often seek discreet corners on the ship but, unfortunately, numerous electric cables for lighting and welding equipment were strewn about the decks. A novice soon learned that the combination of a foot on an exposed 110-volt cable, a wet deck, a supporting grip on a steel rail and pee caused a faster reflex reaction than the warning, 'There's a hat coming up the gangway!' It was definitely an experience not to be repeated!

There were other disadvantages to working on the boats – the incessant background of deafening, brain- and body-numbing noise from the riveters and caulking machines; the welders' blinding white flashes, which were a hazard to other trades (getting a welder's flash could cause days off work with severe migraine-type headaches); and the overall miserable conditions were something of a nightmare. Danger was never distant either. When working on an open deck one day, I was struck by a plank carelessly dropped from a higher level, but thankfully I escaped with only bruising.

I soon settled into the new routine with my affable joiner mate, Harry Beck – who was often taunted with the remark, 'I see Harry's back!' Our primary work was to mark off on the bare expanses of steel decks the positions of welded lugs which would support the wooden bulkheads of the cabins to be erected later for the tanker's crews.

A more unpleasant and much harder job was 'scrunting', where newly-laid wooden decks fitted by the shipwrights had to be scraped using a sharp L-shaped tool, on bended knees for hours at a time. It was a job that was always allocated to apprentices. The task was even more unpleasant when the areas of deck used by workers to relieve themselves also had to be scrunted.

Despite the conditions and hazards, I loved my new workplace. Working in grim conditions on a raw vessel on the building slips was a heady mixture of hard work and adventure. I was amazed that the army of men with their diverse skills could work among each other in apparent chaos and eventually produce a fine ship that would one day carry crews and cargoes to places far away from Belfast. These ships would travel all over the world, to destinations that a yard man could only dream about.

The introduction to the language of shipbuilding was also a revelation – Heater Boys and Catch Boys (when the 'boys' were often forty years old at least), Holders On, White Men (who insulated internal pipes with asbestos lagging), Caulkers (who worked in such close proximity to the loud caulking machines that they were all almost deaf, and tended to shout rather than speak), Tinkers (sheet metal workers), Monkey Islands (dedicated wooden compounds housing the ship's compass), and many more bewildering references soon became part of everyone's working vocabulary.

There was also the rare freedom to wander around the other yards in the vast Queen's Island complex during my (unofficially) extended lunch breaks. There were launches to see; descents to be made down perilous 60-foot ladders into other ships' engine rooms; and one day I climbed to the top of HMS *Eagle*'s superstructure to survey in amazement the massive flight deck stretched out far below. There were other fascinating discoveries – the various gambling groups under the keels of ships on the slipways, or, only yards away, little devout religious groups engaged in worship. Occasionally in the Abercorn Yard, or from other yards, news would arrive of serious accidents of men falling off staging, or suffering fatal injuries from dropped crane loads. An apprentice working in Queen's Island soon learned that, in shipbuilding, injury and even death, either caused by accident or carelessness, was a constant companion.

*

On 21 March 1950 the big day inevitably arrived – the launch of ship 1400! All the wooden staging that had hidden the vessel for months was stripped away, revealing a ship painted in the pristine colours of the new owners. The latest addition to the extensive fleet of the British Tanker Company (later to become BP) now had an identity, and the name *British Explorer* was painted boldly on the bows and stern. The prow of the tanker on the landside of the sloping slipways now towered majestically over the yard, proudly exposed to the world as if boasting, 'Look at me!'

The launch was scheduled for the midday high tide (if the wind was favourable) so all morning, squads of shipwrights and riggers, seemingly indifferent to the dangers, knocked away most of the heavy supporting props under the keel, causing the sound of hammering and falling timbers to echo around the Abercorn Yard. Large wooden wedge-shaped cradles (called poppets) had been built around the bows and stern of the vessel and, when the remaining props were demolished, these were the only support. *British Explorer* was now balanced between the two well-tallowed slipways, down which the cradles would guide the ship into the River Lagan. Launches were not without mishaps. In 1939, the aircraft carrier HMS *Formidable* launched itself prematurely and a female spectator was killed in the confusion.

Two piles of heavy chains attached to the hull lay along each side of the slipways. In the Abercorn Basin two tugs stood by to secure the launched ship and prevent it from smashing into the opposite coal quays (which in the distant future would be home to the magnificent Odyssey complex).

The ceremony for the *British Explorer*'s send-off was a modest affair – such a routine tanker did not justify a high-profile launch – but, regardless of the ship's size, a launch at the Queen's Island was always a special occasion and spectator workers from other areas had assembled to view it. All non-essential workmen were removed from the ship as a safety precaution, while the privileged few remaining on board gathered at the prow, waving cheerfully at the spectators far below. The launch platform was decorated with bunting and the corporate flags of both companies, and a nervous apprentice shipwright presented the customary bouquet of flowers to the tanker chairman's wife. After a short speech, which no one outside the platform party heard, she smashed a bottle of champagne onto the ship's bow. She then pulled a lever to initiate the actual launch.

Somewhere beneath the keel, loud grinding noises were heard accompanied by other mysterious, alarming sounds. The few remaining wooden supports crashed to the ground and powerful hydraulic jacks released the front end of the *British Explorer* off the keel. An absolute, expectant silence enveloped the spectators. But nothing happened – the oil tanker seemed locked to its birthplace. I was concerned. Free of all support, was the ship going to topple over on its side before it even met the water, and cause terrible injuries to the watchful crowd? One wag in the crowd yelled, 'It's stuck, give it another bottle!' Then suddenly after an interminable, anxious delay a slight movement of the front cradle was detected. The waiting crowd erupted into a chorus of applause, whistles and shouts – 'She's going. She's going!' Out in the bay the cheering was taken up by the tugs' crews. They shattered the Lagan air with booming foghorns in the traditional welcome to the new vessel.

Very slowly, almost imperceptibly at first, then with gathering speed, the ship moved along the well-greased slipways. The remaining cables snapped like pieces of string and sent out loud gunshot-like reports across the yard. *Explorer*'s stern struck the water first and immediately most of its superstructure was submerged, as if it was going to sink entirely. As she moved faster down the slipways, the piles of chains were dragged along with an alarming clatter and effectively prevented the ship from hurtling into the opposite coal quays.

Soon the entire ship was in the water and still moving. The wooden cradles had collapsed and floated away but would be retrieved and used for a future launch. A mini tidal wave surged up 1400's empty slipways and scattered the spectators as it washed up wooden props, broken planks, sand and other detritus. The waiting tugs quickly secured the tanker, pulling it safely clear of the perilously close coal quays. With the tanker safely launched and under tug control it was prepared for its first trip along the Lagan to its final fit-out berth on Victoria Wharf.

With the launch ritual completed, the ceremonial party departed the scene in limousines for a celebratory lunch in Harlands' management dining room in the Main Offices. The meal that my workmate and I had was considerably more modest – a packed lunch, washed down with tea brewed in a well-blackened Heinz beans can heated over a riveter's fire. By the time lunch was over and we were leaving the Abercorn to make our way to the *British Explorer*'s new location, the overhead cranes were already laying sections of keel on 1400's former slipways for a new vessel.

# THE HATS

Senior ship managers, depending on their personalities, were the subjects of universal fear, ridicule or respect. More usually referred to as 'the Hats' (a hard hat being the traditional trademark of their authority), they operated across the vast shipyard complex. However those who supervised the vessels under construction or fitting out at the various berths were the least popular as they had no fixed routine of inspections, and would suddenly appear on the scene hoping to catch unwary shirkers. But an early warning system among the workforce was usually effective in preventing confrontations.

In the final months of the Second World War, one of the yard's canteens was crowded with foreign sailors, servicemen and a handful of shipyard men who should not have been there since it was out of bounds. Suddenly, one of the staff shouted out, 'Air Raid! Air Raid!' The workers from the Yard, in a well-practised drill, calmly disappeared through a rear exit, out of danger. The other customers, being strangers and therefore unaware of the workers' early warning system, believed that a devastating German attack on the shipyard was imminent. They dived under tables or ran into the street in panic, hoping to find an air-raid shelter. A few minutes later a Hat appeared. Mr McCuig, nicknamed 'Air Raid', had a notorious reputation for hounding workers for misdemeanours. He was bewildered by the scene of panic that met him – the likelihood of another German Blitz was very small – but no one dared to explain.

Long after the war, and until his retirement in 1961, 'Air Raid' continued to be a figure of fear as he attempted to catch offenders. But, despite his fierce reputation, his peers recognised that he was a committed shipbuilder. To him, maintaining Harlands' worldwide reputation for turning out quality ships was of higher priority than courting popularity with the workforce. After his retirement a more friendlier and relaxed style of 'Hat' management emerged.

Jimmy McKinney, a fitter, was promoted to manager grade and donned the eponymous hat. One day a fellow fitter approached him with a query about an allocated task. 'Jimmy...' he started to say, when he was abruptly interrupted by McKinney who gestured towards his hat. 'See that?' he told the hapless fitter, 'I'm a Hat now. Remember that I'm "Jimmy" no more. It's "Mister" from now on.' The advice was taken. Until his retirement, he was always known as 'Mr Jimmy Nomore'.

Although workers railed at times against management, there was an underlying respect for their authority and how it was earned. But when Gaffers and managers crossed the line between fairness and abuse or cruelty, that tolerance disappeared. When the workmen believed that the code of decency had been breached, drastic retribution sometimes followed. One day a joiner named Clifford, who had mild learning difficulties, tried to leave a ship a few minutes before lunchtime to fill his tea can ahead of the normal gangway stampede down to the hot water boilers. On the way he was accosted by a manager who made fun of the confused workman, humiliating him in front of the other workers. Then, in a dramatic flourish, the manager took off his coat and tried to provoke Clifford to a fight on the jetty. Clifford was finally sent back on board the ship, overcome with embarrassment, to join the queue of waiting workers.

Next morning, as the manager and a colleague were standing talking on the jetty, a heavy plank 'accidentally' dropped from a height of more than 50 feet, missed him by inches. If the plank had hit its target, the manager would have been killed.

Such summary justice was not uncommon on the slipways and fitting-out wharves. There was an intense tribal loyalty among workers, so managers who subjected their men to ill-treatment could expect prompt retribution. The weapons were usually steel pipes, planks and other heavy objects that could inflict injury or death when dropped into engine rooms and on to jetties. They were an effective deterrent or warning against repetition of the offence.

Clifford, for his part, was shrewd enough to challenge the occasional workmate who might tease him – 'When I was released from Purdysburn they gave me a certificate to prove I was sane. Let me see your certificate to prove you're not a head case.' Obviously, such a demand could not be met, and often resulted in an apology.

# THE WHITE MEN

A shipyard career was fraught with danger. Falling tools and equipment were a daily hazard for the men working on the slipways; the woodworking machinery in the Joiners' Shop could cause serious injury and loss of limbs if used incorrectly; and the tremendous noise generated by the riveters and caulking machines on the slipways could cause varying degrees of deafness. But one of the most dangerous jobs in the shipyard (although we did not know it at the time) was that of the White Men – the tradesmen who insulated internal pipes with asbestos lagging.

Asbestos was popular among shipbuilders and other manufacturers because it was resistant to fire, heat, electricity and chemical damage and, most importantly, was affordable. Dick McCappin, a former fitter who worked beneath the White Men in the ships' engine rooms described the loose asbestos fibres as being like snow falling around him. There were no safety measures in place for handling asbestos then.

The substance was not recognised as being toxic until the middle of the twentieth century and Asbestosis was then identified as an industrial disease. But the safety measures that were finally introduced came too late for many shipyard workers, who died from cancer and other lung-related diseases after exposure to the deadly asbestos dust. Even more tragically, the wives of the workers affected often suffered the same fate because they had washed the contaminated overalls for years.

Even workers like McCappin, who had not been exposed to the same levels of asbestos as the White Men, suffered from the effects. He contracted a serious chest condition and, after many years of receiving medical treatment without improvement, he has given up hope of a permanent cure.

Massive compensation payments were made to shipyard workers throughout the UK who worked with asbestos, but many claims – including that of Dick McCappin – are still outstanding.

# SS LAS VEGAS!

The 29,600-ton SS *Iberia* was one of four luxury liners built for the P&O shipping line in the 1950s. Costing £6.9 million, it was built to serve on the UK–Australia route. It was one of the largest passenger ships ever built at Queen's Island. Launched on 21 January 1954, the fit out was completed and the liner was handed over to the owners only eight months later, a remarkable achievement in building a vessel of that type.

Bobbie Simmons, a sheet metal worker (or 'tinker'), worked on the *Iberia* right up until its sea trials and handover. He described how the ship had various large public staterooms which would provide numerous leisure activities for passengers when the ship was at sea. At lunchtime in the shipyard, one, or sometimes two, of these staterooms were taken over by the workers and various casino type games were laid out. There were even croupiers in control of play which, depending upon the proximity of payday, could become very intense at times. Gambling was part of life at the shipyards: poker and other card games were enormously popular. Other activities such as Rub a Dub, Crown and Anchor, Pitch and Toss were also carried out in the luxurious, almost-complete accommodation.

The most popular gambling was on horse racing. Around the walls on special stands were displayed the current newspapers' racing pages with that day's runners. The *Irish News* was regarded as the most comprehensive for racing information, and even the staunchest unionist preferred that paper's coverage of racetracks, jockeys and bookies' odds. Alongside the shipyard organisers were non-shipyard bookmakers who had disguised themselves in overalls to avoid suspicion from the authorities. There were also Harlands' workers who, every day and during working hours, ran illegal 'books'. Bobbie Simmons' impression when he first stumbled upon the scene was that he was in a Hollywood film set, or a Las Vegas gambling saloon that had been transported to Belfast.

Other ships in the Queen's Island enjoyed similar gambling facilities on different scales (depending on the ship's size and state of fit out), and if you had a fondness for gambling, or even if you were merely an interested spectator, all this activity was held in a large, warm, comfortable and dry statement room, which was a welcome diversion and was preferable to the same activities on the cold, miserable slipways.

The existence of these gambling rooms was an open secret – the Gaffers would generally keep discreetly out of the way at lunchtime by staying in their temporary offices on the ships. But a greater threat to illegal gambling on shipyard premises were the members of the Harbour Constabulary – the security guards of the Harland & Wolff complex.

Known to the workers as 'Bulkies', the Harbour Police had similar authority to other police forces, including powers of arrest. Their remit extended about one mile either side of the River Lagan, as far away as Whitehead and Bangor, and well into parts of east and north Belfast. Apparently the nickname arose out of a court case involving a shipyard worker caught stealing. When questioned by the judge about the circumstances of the arrest, the constable replied, 'Your Honour, the accused was acting suspicious and he was bulky under his coat.' In no time the name had become part of the yard's lexicon, and the Harbour Police were seldom called anything else – there was just the occasional expletive prefixing the nickname!

Occasionally an organised swoop would be made on a suspect ship. But lookouts would raise the alarm by word of mouth: 'Bulkies! Bulkies!' By the time the police had boarded and found their way around the vessel, all evidence of gambling had vanished – everything safely hidden away. Instead, the Bulkies found up to about a hundred workers lounging about the state rooms, innocently indulging in normal lunchtime activities such as drinking tea, talking or reading newspapers – a scene of reassuring innocence. Whether the police were fooled or not has never been established. It is unlikely that they were. But they had responded to complaints and their official reports could only confirm that there was no evidence of shipyard workers indulging in illegal activities.

As for the *Iberia*, it had a fairly brief career of only eighteen years, and it suffered from constant operational problems – fires, collisions, electrical failures, engine breakdowns, (and on one occasion it even ran aground) – all of which shortened its normal cruising life, and it was withdrawn from service in 1971. A buyer could not be found for it and its final days were spent in a Taiwan ship breakers yard.

# THE BISHOPS

Ships in the middle of fit out were not the only places in the shipyards where men gathered to gamble or play games during their lunch breaks. Whether you were near the slipways or in any one of the various large workshops, a serious darts match could be taking place in one corner, and a gambling school be in progress in another. A group of workmen in deep concentration would bunch together to play a low-stakes game of poker, while another crowd with a preference for, say, gin rummy could be battling over considerably higher stakes. Frequent mild expletives, and groans of disappointment would be heard if a hand was poor; other men would restrain their exuberance and play in total silence, hoping for good luck. Losses and gains would occasionally be expressed in much earthier language and reactions.

But a short distance from any of the gambling groups (and various other activities), a different sort of activity was often taking place – up to a dozen men (and sometimes more), with sweat-stained faces and dirty overalls or dungarees, were solemnly assembled between benches in a religious service. The usual format of the gathering was Bible readings followed by prayers and sometimes a hymn. If the group was of evangelical persuasion, personal testimonies also featured. The sight of these services being held in such close proximity to the card-playing workers, anomalous perhaps to strangers, hardly attracted a second glance from passing workmates. These were normal daily lunchtime events.

The term 'Bishop' was a friendly, regularly used nickname to describe these shipyard Christians, and those familiar with them also claim the group's leaders or pastors were often known as 'Archbishops'. Sadly, though, not everyone was tolerant of the Bishops – Bobbie Simmons, who spent many years in the Sheet Metal Shop, related an encounter he had one day with a friendly mate. Bob was offered a cigarette, which he politely refused. The friend then asked him if he backed horses. 'Afraid not,' Bob replied. The mate, after further interrogation, then demanded with obvious sarcasm, 'Don't tell me you are a Bishop!' Bob replied, 'If you mean, am I a Christian, the answer is yes.' On hearing that, the supposed friend walked away, expressing disgust and contempt, and never spoke to Bob again. It was a cruel, intolerant reaction to another's convictions and particularly to a friend who had quietly practised his faith without proselytising.

At times, the lunchtime break was enlivened by a different kind of religious activity. Every so often, one particular man – who it is believed did not even work in the shipyards – would ride around the shipyard on a tricycle box cart, similar to that used by ice cream vendors. There was a large loudspeaker mounted on the cart and a record player which played loud, rousing hymns. The 'hymns-on-wheels' preacher would cycle around the Sheet Metal Shop and the Engine Works (and he even made an occasional appearance in the Corn Market area of Belfast on a Saturday) making regular stops and distributing religious tracts to anyone willing to accept them. There is no evidence of him ever performing in the Joiners' Shop, however, despite there being a small, but thriving gospel group there.

Understandably, there was little enthusiasm for the cycling evangelist among the gambling groups, especially when the unwanted sacred music interrupted their concentration. A hapless punter with a run of bad luck and mounting losses was unlikely to be impressed by the stirring

rendition of 'Count Your Blessings' when he faced an early
Judgment Day on Friday as he explained to his wife why she
only received a half-week's wages!

# THE DANCING MASTER

'Slow, slow, quick-quick, slow' is a phrase that could have been applied to the work rate of some shipyard employees, who would lounge around until the sudden appearance of a Hat or Gaffer galvanised them into frenetic action. The phrase was, however, more strongly associated with popular band-leader Victor Sylvester and his weekly BBC TV series *Come Dancing* in the 1950s and 60s.

One dedicated fan of the strict tempo dance programme was Jim Megaw, a fellow first-year apprentice joiner. Every lunchtime, on a vacant area of the Joiners' Shop, he would chalk out various dance step formations – the waltz, the foxtrot and the quickstep were the most popular as they were judged suitable for beginners. He would then invite other workers to join him in practising the steps. He led in the 'female' position and, with any willing male partner he could find, glided across the floor, arms outstretched and high in the correct, traditional style. Megaw would also provide the 'music' by humming, whistling or counting in order to maintain an accurate tempo. He often tried, without success, to encourage me to dance, but my interests lay elsewhere.

In the absence of a volunteer partner he would dance alone. It was a bizarre spectacle to witness a man whirling across the floor, arms outstretched as he held his invisible partner! But in the everyday life of Queen's Island it attracted no more surprise than the daily gambling schools or religious services at lunchtimes. Eccentric characters – like 'the Diver' who regularly jumped off an aircraft carrier's high deck into the deep water at Thompson Wharf; or the shipwright who practised on his 'piano' (a wooden painted replica of a keyboard) every day – often earned little more than a passing glance. Sometimes the piano player's mates would distract him by making requests. 'I haven't got the music for that one,' he would respond, as he continued his silent recital.

Most of us were aware of Megaw's dedication to his hobby. We knew that he was attending a dancing school in Belfast, that he entered dancing competitions and that he had even won a bronze medal for his efforts. Sometimes other workers would joke about the dancing but the teasing was always given, and taken, in good spirit.

By the early 1960s Megaw, having left Harlands a few years previously, had progressed from pupil to part-time instructor and demonstrator at the Billy Neely dance studio in Belfast's Ann Street. Shortly after, he and his wife Mary represented Northern Ireland in the regional series of the BBC *Come Dancing* programmes. A greater achievement followed a few years later when the couple won the All-Ireland Waltz Championship. When Billy Neely died, Mrs Neely and Megaw shared ownership and management of the dance studio. It was a thriving arrangement until the onset of the Troubles in 1969. A changing social culture among a young generation also contributed to the ultimate demise of dance schools – many closed down to be eventually replaced by clubs with discos and alcohol licences.

None of us who worked with Jim Megaw in the early years of our apprenticeship could have imagined that his unusual lunchtime behaviour in the Joiners' Shop was a harbinger of the successful and exciting career that lay ahead of him. Such is life!

# THE SHED

In heavy industry there might appear to be few opportunities for workmen to steal from their employers. Harland & Wolff, in the business of building ships with tonnages in the thousands, might seem to be a particularly unlikely source of rich pickings. But the construction of ships, particularly passenger ships fitted out to luxurious standards, could be a thief's paradise – an Aladdin's cave of bathroom fittings, mirrors and other items that were to be used to furnish the cabins of passengers and crew. Any attractive item, providing it could be easily removed and reinstalled in a worker's home, could quickly disappear, leaving a foreman tearing his hair out in frustration, trying to find replacements and having to give an explanation to his superiors.

Pilfering from the Belfast shipyard was no more endemic than elsewhere (although stealing fellow workmen's tools was taboo and seldom occurred). But when over fifteen thousand workers are in an environment with easy access to useful items they cannot afford, some will be unable to resist temptation.

In the days before the Second World War, poverty was widespread and even for those fortunate enough to have a (usually poorly paid) job, daily life was a struggle. Most Belfast shipyard workers lived in back-to-back terraced houses, sparsely furnished and with few amenities. An ex-Harland & Wolff bathroom mirror, in a house with only a tin bath in front of a coal fire, gave at least a semblance of luxury.

Little was sacrosanct to the workers who were keen to obtain something for nothing. Materials such as company tools, paint, wood and fittings were very popular, as was the creation of homer projects. In the month of June a favourite acquisition was red paint. Practically overnight, hundreds of Belfast houses would have a fresh coat of red paint on the lower half of their front walls – decorated just in time for the Twelfth of July holidays. It was not difficult to ascertain where the residents of some homes worked.

One story I heard was of a shipyard worker who was off sick and had his weekly wages brought to the home by a friendly workmate. As the friend entered the house and looked around to take in the contents (most of which had belonged to Harlands), he immediately burst out: 'My God! When's this ship going to be launched?'

Low-profile pilfering by workers was a feature over many generations in the yard, often carried out by those who would not consider lifting an apple from an unattended stall outside a fruit shop, or a turnip from a farmer's field. But in the early 1920s an unusual sequence of events took place at Queen's Island – workmen began returning the shipyard goods that they had stolen over the years. Among them were huge items that, somehow, had been smuggled past the keen surveillance of the Harbour Police manning the Queens Road and Dee Street security gates.

The catalyst for the sudden change of heart was an Ulster evangelist, William Patteson Nicholson, often referred to as WPN. The threats of hell, fire and brimstone were his weapons of choice, while 'God's Love' and 'God's Hell' were favourite themes. His pulpit style was earthy and verged on vulgarity and crudeness, but he made no apologies for this. His mission was to save souls, and the ends justified the means.

During one memorable service a drunk in the audience began to cause a disruption, so Nicholson grabbed the culprit by the scruff of the neck and pitched him out of the church. A woman criticised him: 'Mr Nicholson, our Saviour wouldn't have done that.' 'No,' said the preacher, 'he would have cast the devil out of the man. I cannot do that, madam, so I did the second-best thing. I cast out the man and the devil as well.'

Despite a down-to-earth pulpit manner, which often distressed many in his audiences, thousands were converted by him and retained their faith over their lifetimes – it is widely acknowledged that Nicholson made a major contribution to the spiritual revival movement that swept Britain and the world in the 1920s and 1930s.

His mass public meetings were attended by many industrial workers, including shipyard men, and the unemployed, and in his own way Nicholson helped to shape society by laying down standards of behaviour in a period when poverty could exert severe strain on morality. The preacher, despite his uncouth disposition, managed to bring comfort and hope to countless people, giving them reassurance about a better hereafter. It is recognised that the presence of hundreds of Nicholson's converts in the shipyards – men who had become dedicated practising Christians – exercised a powerful moderating influence, particularly in the aftermath of Irish partition in 1921. Inter-community tensions in Northern Ireland were at a high, often violent level in the 1920s. A violent IRA refusal to accept the political settlement, and the reluctance of the Roman Catholic hierarchy and some of its adherents to recognise the legitimacy of the new Stormont regime, clashed with the fears of the Protestant majority, still insecure in their new constitutional status. In the volatile political situation all the elements for a potential civil war were present. The Belfast shipyards, with a mixed Catholic and Protestant workforce, could not escape the sectarian tensions that arose after partition, but thanks in part to WPN and his followers, the bitter sectarian hostilities did not spiral out of control, and commercial and civil anarchy in the shipyards, with a possible loss of lives, was narrowly averted.

Apart from emphasising repentance from sin, WPN forcefully advocated restitution for previous misdeeds against fellow men. It was the spur that alerted the shipyard workers to past wrongdoings. In 1923, after a series of highly emotive meetings in which restitution was encouraged, pilfered goods began to make their way back to astonished employers.

One business owner in Lisburn wrote to Nicholson expressing gratitude for his influence and claimed that others he knew were also having their stolen goods returned. But the most dramatic results were in the Belfast shipyards of Harland & Wolff and Workman Clark. The volume of returned items was so huge that Harlands erected a dedicated warehouse to store the stolen tools and other items. When the 'Nicholson Shed,' as it was called, was filled to capacity, the Yard management had to issue this urgent appeal – 'Will those attending the meetings of Mr William Patteson Nicholson please stop returning stolen goods? We have nowhere to store them.'

# THE SANDWICH MEN

A yardman's lunch was usually simple fare – a home-made sandwich (a 'piece') carried in a tin box along with another small, double-ended container which held tea and sugar. The sandwich fillings were, for the most part, very basic (cooked ham being the most popular), but there were a few exceptions.

A fellow apprentice joiner, Jimmy Donaghy from Ligoneil, regularly brought in raw cabbage sandwiches which he generously offered to share, though there were few takers! Donaghy was a Catholic, but each June he would go around the squad collecting donations to decorate the benches in the Joiners' Shop in time for the Twelfth of July holidays. No one was sure why he did this but, as he was a popular character, he was given the benefit of any doubt. Eventually he left the Yard and moved to America, where he joined the New York Police Department. If his lunchtime habits had not changed it is possible his tough American colleagues might have had misgivings about their own Irish ancestry when this cabbage-eating Irishman joined their ranks.

Another character, from the Woodstock Road in Belfast, had equally exotic tastes. He acquired the nickname Popeye, as twice a week he would bring in spinach sandwiches. When questioned about his tastes he would, in all seriousness, explain that there was proven scientific evidence that spinach aided muscle development and good body tone. That may have been the case, but few of the other workers ever saw him put those muscles to good use in lifting anything heavier than his pay on a Friday.

Lunchtime aboard a fitting-out ship was a different

routine from that in the confined spaces of a workshop. Aboard ship most workers would enjoy lunch in close proximity, sitting around on toolboxes at improvised tables which had been knocked together from spare bits of wood. The more fastidious would lay a newspaper on the 'table' as a table cloth and carefully spread their victuals on it – sugar, milk, the well-burned Heinz can of freshly brewed tea and the sandwiches which were always neatly wrapped in paper. It was a procedure that would have delighted any restaurant proprietor. Such workers usually had the best lunches, and were always subject to furtive glances from others, curious about the contents of their mate's lunchbox. They would even experience unwelcome approaches from other envious diners.

One incident often related, possibly as a warning to others, involved a fitter who seldom brought in a lunch as either he or his wife were too lazy to make one up. He would regularly scrounge from any worker who displayed an appetising piece. On some occasions the irritable owner of the sandwich would burst out, 'Why don't you take the whole bloody lot?' The rhetorical invitation was taken literally and the fitter would unashamedly eat his colleague's entire lunch without batting an eyelid. When this practice became more than a minor nuisance, two workmen plotted to take action. One was given specific instructions: 'Tomorrow, bring in plain sandwiches with no fillings and a bottle of ketchup. We'll sort out this bugger once and for all.' Next day when the workman arrived with the plain sandwiches, the other accomplice produced four dead mice. He cut off the tails and chopped the bodies, including the heads, into small pieces and placed them between the bread. He completed the filling with a liberal covering of ketchup. That lunch break, the scrounger sidled up to the workman who had laid the sandwiches out on his table. 'Those are very tasty-looking sandwiches you have today. Your wife takes good care of you. Wish I was so lucky. Do you mind if I try one?' 'Not at all,' said the owner, 'take the lot if you like. I'm not hungry today.' He quickly devoured the sandwiches and gave the compliment, 'Those are the best sandwiches I've enjoyed for a long time. They have an unusual flavour but are still very tasty. Your wife must have a good butcher.' The actual 'butcher', who had been standing nearby, tapped the fitter on the shoulder. 'Do you realise what you've just eaten, mate? Four dead mice fillings. Would you like the same tomorrow again?' The fitter instantly became violently sick, bringing up the recent sandwiches and his breakfast as well. With a string of expletives directed towards his mates, he disappeared at speed from the scene and was not seen at work for three days. When he did return, he was carrying a brand new lunchbox – his first – and dined alone.

A similar occurrence took place on another ship. On that occasion the victim found that the sausage sandwich he had scrounged from a friendly workmate had actually been doctored with a length of steel welding rod. Several broken teeth cured him of his antisocial habits.

Those actual incidents are reminiscent of a story that circulated in the shipyard for a time but which is probably apocryphal as the source was never authenticated. Three workmen sat together during their lunch breaks and sometimes discussed or shared their pieces. Two of the men always had a variety of tasty fillings, while the other invariably had corned beef. One day he threw his lunch away in disgust. 'That's it,' he said. 'I've had enough of that garbage. If I get corned beef one more time I'll throw myself over the edge of this ship.' Next day, during the lunch break, the workmen unwrapped their lunches and the frustrated workman's piece was again corned beef. Without hesitation, he leapt from the top deck into the water far below and drowned. One of his companions remarked, 'That was a drastic, stupid reaction over a mere sandwich.' 'You're absolutely right,' said his mate, 'especially when he always makes up his own piece.'

# THE MISSING BATH

One talent that yardmen had to acquire early in their career was that of improvisation and quick thinking in embarrassing situations. My father, Jack, was a plumber's helper and he would often tell me of the time when he and Porky Brown, a plumber, returned to complete a nearly-finished passenger cabin they had fitted out the previous day. They obtained the cabin keys from the Key Man – a joiner who secured all cabins in an advanced stage of fit out to prevent pilfering – but when they entered the room they were shocked to find a large crack in the bath they had installed earlier.

Porky was aghast, 'Some careless bugger has dropped a spanner in it and we'll get the blame.'

'What can we do about it?' asked my father. 'The Gaffer's not going to believe we're innocent.'

But Porky had a sudden brainwave. 'Never worry, leave it to me. Go and find Briggsy, the shipwright, and borrow his twenty-pounder.'

My father eventually located the shipwright and obtained the sledgehammer. Porky issued new instructions: 'Close the door, stay outside and keep a lookout for anyone coming along.' From the closed cabin my father could hear a succession of bangs and crashing noises, punctuated with grunts. When the door reopened, the floor was littered with pieces of broken porcelain. 'Open the porthole, Jack,' ordered Porky. 'If no one sees it then we can't be blamed.' They then tipped all the fragments of the bath, piece by piece, into the Musgrave Channel. There was no evidence that the cabin had ever had a bath. 'Now, go and fetch the Gaffer,' said Porky.

When the Gaffer arrived, Porky showed him the vacant

bath space and complained, 'We spent a whole day yesterday installing a bath. Look there it is – gone. When we arrived this morning we discovered that some bugger had stolen it. How he got it off the ship and past the watchman beats me.'

The Gaffer's response was sympathetic: 'He probably gave a crane man a few bob and it was lifted on to a lorry. But I'm going to have a word with the Key Man. He's obviously getting too careless about who he's handing keys to.'

Next day the hapless Key Man, who had been severely reprimanded for lax security, reluctantly opened the cabin to allow Porky and Jack to install a replacement bath.

Porky later commented, 'It disgusts me the number of devious men who work in the shipyard. The careless bugger who cracked our bath hadn't the guts or decency to admit liability, so others have to pick up the pieces.'

'You're absolutely right there, mate – the pieces are now at the bottom of the Musgrave Channel,' my father quietly reminded him.

# THE LADDER

Ernie Wilson shook his head in disbelief, 'You'll never get that bloody monster of a thing past the Bulkies on the Queens Road gates. They would have to be blind to miss it. Could you not have made something smaller that you could have stuffed up your jacket?'

The subject of Ernie's concern was a recently completed 12-foot ladder concealed under the long joiners' workbench he shared with his mate Andy. The ladder was a superb specimen of the craftsmanship for which Harland & Wolff was renowned. It was made from Burmese teak, notoriously difficult to work with, and the most expensive of wood, but noted for its durability in all climatic extremes. It was widely used by shipyards around the world for external woodwork exposed to the elements.

Harlands could be depended upon to use only the best quality materials for their ships. Likewise, Andy, a timber connoisseur, would only use the best for his homer projects. His ladder was a masterpiece, a labour of love: curved, flawlessly smooth uprights; every third rung reinforced with thick welders' rods for extra strength; and – the *pièce de résistance* – rubber suction pads at each end to prevent slipping.

Its construction had taken place surreptitiously over two weeks during Andy's lunch breaks. Doing homers was a decidedly risky activity, particularly under the tight regime in the vast Joiners' Shop where the Charge Hands or Gaffers rigorously supervised their sections, monitoring workmanship or looking out for joiners on the skive. But the creation of homers was a practice particularly frowned upon by shipyard management. If anyone was caught exploiting the yards' materials and time, retribution was swift and ruthless – in extreme cases resulting in prosecution and prison. Workers, however, had an effective early warning system in place, and few were ever caught red-handed. If Jimmy McGrath, the Head Foreman, or Sir Frederick Rebbeck, the Managing Director, were sighted on one of their regular tours, a shout or a piece of wood landing on the offender's bench from another worker, acted as a warning signal.

But Ernie was still concerned and curious about his mate's long ladder. 'Never mind the risk getting it home,' he commented to Andy, 'why do you want a 12-foot ladder?' Andy, who was normally reticent about his illegal activities, explained, 'It's for my new pigeon loft, which is higher and replaces the one blown down last winter.'

Days of speculation followed about how Andy could smuggle his ladder – the largest homer anyone could remember – past the Harbour Police. Andy would only smile and say, with a finger tapped knowingly on the side of his head, 'You leave that to me, mate. I know what I'm doing.' A few fellow joiners, in frustration, suggested that the tapping his head gesture was a sure sign that perhaps Andy had a serious mental problem and should be restrained before he did something stupid. They worried that Andy could lose his job, or even finish up in Crumlin Road Jail.

But wiser minds knew their man – over the years, Andy had proved a skilled tactician in getting numerous homers safely past the police. Miniature grand pianos which played nursery rhymes when the lid was raised, bathroom cabinets, piano stools and a folding table were among his achievements. Andy's techniques for getting items past the eagle-eyed Bulkies were not unique to him. At knocking-off time, many limping workers, with items hidden in their trousers, or others, standing very erect and suspiciously flat-chested, somehow escaped the notice of the police. A popular dodge was for a worker to purchase a cheap piece of wood from Hamilton Bodel's timber yard on Sydenham Road at lunchtime. The worker then altered the receipt and brandished it at the Harbour Police – while carrying a bundle of stolen wood – at knocking-off time. The Bulkies only cursorily studied the receipt, if they bothered looking at all.

As the time for the ladder's exit from the Yard drew nearer, speculation among the other joiners was reaching a high pitch, with Andy concerned that the gossip would reach the ears of Leslie, their Gaffer. Otherwise he remained unfazed, expressing irritation rather than fear when he learned that the Harbour Police had been reinforced at the security gates. His only reaction was, 'That's because of some greedy buggers on the *Pretoria Castle*. They stole two newly installed baths, a pedestal wash-hand basin and a pile of fittings. All they've done is make life more difficult for decent people like ourselves.'

The following Monday, Andy made his move, with the timing and tactics well prepared in advance. At 3.30 p.m. Andy gave a first year apprentice a half-crown tip to throw his time board into the timekeeper's hut at quitting time so that, although absent, he would suffer no loss of wages. The next step was to have a word with his Gaffer: 'Sorry, Leslie, I have to leave early – not feeling well at all. Probably a touch of food poisoning. I blame a bad fish supper I got last night. Do you mind if I pack my tools and head off home?' Andy, with his leave of absence sympathetically approved, returned to his bench to await a suitable opportunity. Minutes later the Gaffer disappeared into his office for his afternoon tea-break. Wasting no time, Andy extracted the ladder from its well-concealed position under the bench. His workmates and others in the adjacent sections ceased work, and stood open-mouthed in amazement as he boldly carried the ladder, shoulder high, along the aisles between the work sections. He made an exit from the Joiners' Shop via the side doors which led into the rear yard.

The next stop was the bicycle shed. Nearby was a fire bucket which had had its sand replaced with water. With the ladder balanced across his bicycle and the bucket slung on a handlebar Andy headed for home. Like many other famous Harland & Wolff constructions, the ladder was leaving its birthplace!

He wheeled the bicycle and its load along the Queens Road past the main offices and Engine Works. It was a tiring, half-mile journey from the Joiners' Shop to the planned rendezvous point. About fifty yards from the Harbour gates, Andy unhitched his load. He placed the ladder against the nearest office block and, using cloths from the bicycle satchel bag and the bucket of water, he proceeded to clean the windows. As he progressed from one building to another along the Queens Road, the distance to the Harbour gates decreased. His suspicions were confirmed. Instead of just one, there were now two Bulkies on duty, one on each side of the road. They were carefully scrutinising the early leaving traffic and workers. When Andy had reached the offices nearest to the gates, and had cleaned the windows, he stopped for a break, rested against the bicycle, and lit a cigarette. The policeman approached him, looking menacing, as they were prone to do. 'You'll not get much work done sitting on your backside like that,' he said in an admonishing but friendly tone of voice. A flow of convivial conversation ensued between the two men. Andy switched over to his complaining mode: 'I wouldn't mind your job

– well paid for just standing about all day. This window cleaning lark is not paying at all, and with two falls already it's just not worth it. Are there any vacancies in the Harbour Police, Sergeant?' (The policeman was clearly a constable but Andy knew that addressing lower-rank policemen in such a manner was a good move.) 'Forget about it, son,' came the response, 'you'd have to grow another foot – you wouldn't meet the minimum height requirement. Another thing, for your information, we don't just stand about all day doing nothing. This is a very stressful job. Vigilance is our motto. You have no idea of the stealing that goes on in the shipyard. My ambition is to catch some of the really big operators one day and put them well away, up the Crumlin Road Jail.' Andy mused whether he and his long ladder might fit into the category of a big-time criminal.

'Is that so? I find that hard to believe. Anyhow, I'm off now. Done enough before the Yard gets out, the rush begins and I get knocked off my ladder again.' After a cheery farewell to the policeman, who advised him to watch the traffic, Andy gathered his equipment and moved on to the next building outside the Harbour gates. He cleaned a few more windows as he made his way towards Station Street until, safely out of sight of the Bulkies, he abandoned the redundant bucket and headed home. Mission accomplished.

Two weeks later, without an explanation for his workmates or Gaffer, Andy handed in his notice. Rumours circulated that he had been caught at last in another shipyard escapade.

About ten years later, Ernie, then retired, bumped into his former mate in a Belfast pub. Andy exuded confidence and prosperity. He was expensively dressed and carried a briefcase – a marked contrast to Andy the joiner with his soiled, torn apron. After the initial greetings, Ernie, to avoid asking obvious embarrassing questions inquired, 'Are you still racing pigeons, Andy?' His old friend was aghast at the question. 'Most definitely not. I soon caught on that keeping and feeding them, as well as having to clean up after them, would never make me any money. If my birds did win a race, all I got was a cheap plastic trophy, and if I was lucky, a photograph in the *Pigeon Weekly*. Big deal! My old job as wood butcher in the Joiners' Shop for twelve pounds a week was no catch either. Today I'm self-employed with twenty-eight men working for me, and seven vehicles on the road. Since I saw you last I've made a fortune and been enjoying life to the full, with holiday homes in Monaco and Florida. But business has its ugly moments too sometimes. Last week I had to sack two workers. Would you believe it the buggers were abusing my trust for their own personal gain.'

Ernie, still puzzled, had to ask, 'Andy, what is your business?'

'Do you remember the time I smuggled a ladder out from the Joiners' Shop? "Not possible!" you all said, and I proved you wrong. Well it inspired me to start up a window-cleaning business. At present I have hundreds of contracts for Belfast offices, with good clients and payments on the button. And it's all run from my posh offices at the back of the City Hall in just two hours a day. The rest of the time I play golf. But last week I was livid when I found out that some of my staff were using my equipment, and in my time, to do private jobs and were pocketing the money. There was no other option than sack them. There's no bloody loyalty or integrity in workers anymore.'

Ernie, shocked, could only agree. 'You are absolutely right, Andy. It was never like that in our day.'

# THE DIAGONAL STEAM TRAP

Now they built a big ship down in Harlands
She was made for to sell to the Turks
And they called on the yard's chief designer
To design all the engines and works.

Now finally the engines was ready
And they screwed in the very last part
An' yer man says, 'Let's see how she runs, lads!'
An' bejasus! the thing wouldn't start!

So they pushed and they worked an' they footered
An' the engineers' faces got red
The designer he stood lookin' stupid
An' scratchin' the back o' his head.

But while they were fiddlin' and workin'
Up danders oul' Jimmy Dalzell
He had worked twenty years in the Island
And ten in the aircraft as well.

So he pushed and he worked and he muttered
Till he got himself through to the front
And he has a good look roun' the engine
An' he gives a few mutters and grunts,

And then he looks up at the Gaffer
An' says he 'Mr Smith, d'ye know?
They've left out the Diagonal Steam Trap!
How the hell d'ye think it could go?'

Now the engineer eyed the designer
The designer he looks at the 'Hat'
And they whispered the one to the other
'Diagonal Steam Trap? What's that?'

But the Gaffer, he wouldn't admit, like
To not knowin' what this was about,
So he says 'Right enough, we were stupid!
The Diagonal Steam Trap's left out!'

Now in the meantime oul' Jimmy had scarpered
Away down to throw in his boord
And the Gaffer comes up and says 'Jimmy!
D'ye think we could have a wee word?

Ye see that Diagonal Steam Trap?
I know it's left out – it's bad luck
But the engine shop's terrible busy
D'ye think ye could knock us one up?'

Now, oul' Jimmy was laughin' his scone off
He had made it all up for a gag
He'd seen what was stoppin' the engine –
The feed-pipe was blocked with a rag!

But he sticks the oul' hands in the pockets
An' he says 'Aye, I'll give yez a han'!
I'll knock yes one up in the mornin'
An' the whole bloody thing will be grand!'

So oul' Jim starts to work the next morning
To make what he called a Steam Trap,
An oul' box an' a few bits of tubing
An' a steam gauge stuck up on the top,

An' he welds it all on to the engine
And he says to the wonderin' mob
'As long as that gauge is at zero
The Steam Trap is doin' its job!'

Then he pulls the rag outta the feed pipe
An' he gives the oul' engine a try
An' bejasus! she goes like the clappers
An' oul' Jimmy remarks 'That's her nye!'

Now the ship was the fastest seen ever
So they sent her away to the Turks
But they toul' them 'That Steam Trap's a secret!
We're the only ones knows how it works!'

But the Turks they could not keep their mouths shut
An' soon the whole story got roun'
An' the Russians got quite interested ...
Them boys has their ears to the groun'!

So they sent a spy dressed as a sailor
To take photies of Jimmy's Steam Trap
And they got them all back to the Kremlin
An' they stood round to look at the snaps.

Then the head spy says 'Mr Kosygin!
I'm damned if I see how that works!'
So they sent him straight off to Siberia
An' they bought the whole ship from the Turks!

When they found the Steam Trap was a 'cod', like,
They couldn't admit they'd been had
So they built a big factory in Moscow
To start makin' Steam Traps like mad!

Then Kosygin rings up Mr Nixon
And he says 'Youse'uns thinks yez are great!
But wi' our big new Russian-made Steam Trap
Yez'll find that we've got yez all bate!'

Now oul' Nixon, he nearly went 'harpic'
So he thought he'd give Harlands a call
And he dialled the engine-shop number
And of course he got sweet bugger all!

But at last the call came through to Jimmy
In the midst of a terrible hush,
'There's a call for you here, from the White House!'
Says oul' Jim, 'That's a shop in Portrush!'

There's a factory outside of Seattle
Where they're turnin' out Steam Traps like Hell
It employs twenty-five thousand workers
And the head of it ... Jimmy Dalzell!

*Crawford Howard*

'The Diagonal Steam Trap' by Crawford Howard can justifiably be hailed as the best well-known popular poem to originate in Belfast: a shipyard poem that is celebrated well beyond Ulster's shores. When it is recited, audiences of all backgrounds seldom fail to respond with enthusiasm, however often it has been heard. The poem's hilarious absurdity can be interpreted as satirical commentary on the gullibility and vanity of people, including those in authority, when prestige is all-important.

Crawford Howard, although credited with the 'Steam Trap' and many other humorous verses, has remained an elusive, enigmatic figure. Now enjoying a quiet retirement, he lives in the same Belfast street where he was born eighty-five years ago. His early education was at Inst (RBAI) followed by Trinity College, Dublin, where he studied languages. A fellow student, who became a good friend, was the son of a Harland & Wolff manager. Howard often visited his friend's home in Belfast. The young men, dressed in workers' overalls, would wander unchallenged around the vast shipyard complex, talking to workmen and exploring the various ships berthed at the fitting-out jetties. On occasion, Howard, who had a sound basic knowledge of electronics, would carry out installation work on simple circuits and other electrical tasks – entirely without authorisation – but apparently competently. Over that period he absorbed the ethos and working conditions of a major shipbuilding industry. He also shared the camaraderie and experiences of the men who made Queen's Island a world leader in workmanship.

In his school days, Howard discovered a talent for composing humorous poetry mainly about teachers and other pupils. 'It was only doggerel,' he claims, modestly, though his teenage scribbling would one day lead to fame and give regular pleasure to many. An accomplished performer on the tin whistle, for a time he played regularly with the Glen Folk Four – 'Sometimes it was the Glen Folk Six!'. John Bennett, the BBC personality, was on guitar; Vincent Hanna, the political analyst, did the vocals; and on occasions, 'Mr Banjo' Jimmy Gillespie, or other guest artists played with them. Long before joining the folk group, Howard had been writing humorous poems, mainly for his own amusement, with the occasional impromptu performances for friends or at social functions. Most of the credit for lifting Crawford Howard out of the obscurity he preferred is due to Calum of the Tommy and Calum Sands Folk Duo. They had heard him performing one evening at the Arts Club, Belfast. Impressed by his act (monologues, tin whistle and singing) they invited him onto their Downtown radio show. It was a debut that raised his public profile higher than he would have chosen. The Sands duo later persuaded him to make a recorded collection of his poems, and several were set to well-known tunes. Some of the material highlighted the tribal prejudices of republican and loyalist traditions but without rancour or bitterness. Howard explained, 'These songs can be sung anywhere. The political angle is submerged in the humour.' The 'Steam Trap' poem in particular, with the Belfast shipyard theme, can be seen as a work of industrial satire which is applicable to many other situations.

The collection was released on cassette tape and launched in the Harland & Wolff Welders Club in the 1980s. It became a resounding bestseller and was subsequently re-issued on CD. Such was his modesty, that it was only when the original record was released and received significant radio airtime, that his colleagues (at the Pig Marketing Board) were alerted to his talent and fame .

Over thirty years later, Howard's poems continue to

appear in print, and his CDs – including a compilation album, *Diagonal Steam Trap: The Worst of Crawford Howard* – still sell steadily. Howard, at this late stage of his life may no longer enjoy the recognition and fame he once received but his writings, with their rich mixture of satire, whimsy and observation, have a unique quality of social comment which, through warts-and-all humour, portrays the essential Belfast man's character. Circulated during the most violent period in Northern Ireland's history, his poetry and humour helped in a small way to lighten the despair, and prove that – even in a bitter, divided community – when each side could share a laugh at their own, and others', prejudices, there was hope for the future.

Perhaps that is tribute enough to Crawford Howard, the 'Shipyard Man Who Never Was'.

# KILROY

In the 1940s and 1950s, there was one particular figure who was more recognisable around the shipyard than Sir Frederick Rebbeck, the Managing Director – Kilroy. Despite his popularity and frequent sightings of him across the entire Queen's Island complex, Kilroy always remained an elusive and enigmatic character, more mischievous and irritating than any of the yard's other eccentric personalities. Although conspicuous in even the farthest corners of the shipyard, no one had ever actually met him. In the early days, when he first began to appear, he was a source of concern and frustration among the workforce. Was he an undercover surveillance agent acting on behalf of the management? Was there an even more sinister explanation?

In fact, Kilroy was no flesh-and-blood personality. He was entirely fictional – a harmless cartoon character of no particular significance, who posed no threat to anyone. He was always depicted in a crude chalk or crayon sketch as a wide-eyed, bald-headed figure peering over a wall or fence. His long nose would hang over the wall, and he was almost always accompanied by the caption, 'Kilroy was here!' His enigmatic face would appear on ships' bulkheads, workshop walls and, inevitably, toilet blocks but eventually the mysterious graffiti began to extend beyond the shipyard into other industries and buildings around Belfast.

In certain locations the crude doodle with the inane caption was a welcome, reassuring spectacle to Harlands workers. An essential, unpleasant task for some trades was working in the restricted heights and claustrophobic spaces of a ship's double bottoms, where workers were unable to stand upright and often had to crawl to move around. They spent most of their time in darkness with the only illumination coming from their standard-issue red candles. Rats tended to infest that part of the ship, scurrying around the workmen's feet as they worked through the long tunnels. Being confronted by a huge threatening rat, or the decomposing remains of poisoned vermin, was a frequent and unnerving experience. But a glimpse of Kilroy prominently chalked on steel plating and looming out of the semi darkness, in that unpleasant, remote place, offered reassurance that someone had been there before and had presumably survived the grim, dangerous conditions.

In a different context, away from the Queen's Island, a particular group of men found little humour in the obtrusive cartoon. A gang of thieves broke into a business premises in Belfast but when they successfully opened the safe and cash boxes they were shocked to find that others had beaten them to it and all valuables had already been stolen. All that remained was a sketch of a certain bald-headed character with the taunting note, 'Hard luck. Kilroy was here!'

The men of Harlands had presumed that the Kilroy phenomenon had originated at the Belfast shipyard since his appearances there were so widespread. But when we heard reports of him turning up at other British shipyards, we realised that the source might lie elsewhere, somewhere with a shipbuilding connection.

It is now accepted that the original source was at the Quincy shipyard, Massachusetts, USA. An inspector named J.J. Kilroy would chalk up the slogan, 'Kilroy was here!' to indicate approval for any work completed. It is assumed that a local wit could not resist embellishing the comment with the cartoon character depicting the same inspector peering all around to highlight correct workmanship. During the Second World War, the Kilroy cartoon and caption appeared on war materials wherever American Air Transport Command was active. When the name Kilroy was found on captured US equipment, German intelligence suspected that it referred to a high-level secret agent. Stalin also was convinced that it referred to vital military information that the Allies were withholding from him. His investigations inevitably came to nothing.

Hundreds of thousands of US service men passed through Northern Ireland during the war and, as a result, we experienced both a military and a cultural invasion. Chewing gum, nylons, new dances and other expressions of a different culture became part of mainstream Ulster society. Many of the Yanks entered through or worked in the vicinity of the Belfast Harbour area, and it is possible that they were the importers of the all-pervading Kilroy character.

There is some historical evidence that there was a similar contemporary cartoon character which was of British origin. 'Mr Chad' was a wide-eyed, bald-headed man with a long nose, who would look over a wall and mutter (amongst other things), 'Wot! No beer!?' Or, 'Wot! No cigarettes!?' Created in 1938 by a newspaper cartoonist, Chad was very popular with American forces during the war and was said to have been used as humorous relief in difficult situations. In the war years and for a period afterwards, both Kilroy and Mr Chad were in popular usage around Northern Ireland. Although the doodles largely died out, the characters acquired a universal appeal and still appear on buildings throughout the world with the caption in the local language. A piece of the Berlin wall with the Kilroy cartoon was salvaged and is today in an American museum.

At present, memories of those baffling characters which

decorated the Belfast shipyard survive among the older generation. Like much of the other folklore that is part of the Queen's Island history, Mr Chad and Kilroy made their bizarre contribution to an industrial culture which consisted of much more than merely building fine ships.

# BILLY HULK!

Billy Hull – a stocky, heavyweight, Shankill Road man – was Trade Union Shop Steward and Convener in the Engine Works. Like many of his class and generation, his education was minimal, as he had left school at fourteen years of age. An unsophisticated, straight-speaking Belfast character, he performed his union duties effectively and enjoyed the confidence of his fellow members.

A Convener's responsibilities in the shipyard were always ambiguous. Although employed to work full-time as tradesmen, their official trade union status also meant that the employer had to provide reasonable time off for them to mediate workplace disputes (which were often about demarcation between different trades, or working conditions). In actual fact, Conveners spent little time on their job and would still receive a full week's pay. It was the ideal job, as a Convener could wander around the Yard without hindrance or having to account to any authority.

A new opportunity for Hull's union skills came in 1971 when he helped to establish the Loyalist Association of Workers (LAW). As well as its strong links with the Ulster Defence Association (UDA), LAW had evolved from an earlier political organisation, the Workers' Committee for the Defence of the Constitution, which had campaigned against IRA violence and the threat to Ulster's position within the UK. LAW had a strong base in the shipyard, mainly due to Hull's influence, and support was also growing at the aircraft factory of Short & Harland. LAW assumed a higher public profile in 1972 when the Stormont Parliament was abolished. It became closely associated with William Craig's Vanguard

Unionist Party which began an active campaign against the suspension of Stormont.

Billy Hull as Joint Chairman of LAW was a regular spokesman on the news for the organisation. But it was soon obvious, through no fault of his own, that he did not have the articulate and persuasive authority that one would expect from a group that planned to extend its power base beyond the working-class community. As a result, while membership of LAW did increase, it was mainly concentrated around factories in the greater Belfast area.

However, it was when the popular Ulster comedian James Young created a parody of Hull that his public persona really suffered. From 1972 to 1973 Young had a popular TV series, *Saturday Night,* which was transmitted on Saturday evenings on the BBC and which was hugely successful across Northern Ireland. Young's talent was his ability to caricature well-known, recognisable local stereotypes. Orange Lil, Mrs McConaghy, The Lady from Cherryvalley and others were all accurate (but grossly exaggerated) portrayals of Northern Irish characters. One of Young's characters was Billy Hulk, a shipyard shop steward who puffed away on a cigarette butt-end and delivered forceful, expert opinions on topical issues of the day. The mannerisms and personality of Hulk clearly pointed to the real public figure, and when Hull appeared as a spokesman in the media for LAW, many in the audience naturally saw Young's spoof character. Billy Hull's reputation suffered.

LAW, in the meantime was suffering from its own bad publicity – on 7 February 1973 LAW and the Vanguard Party held a 'Day of Action' when electricity supplies were stopped in Belfast; a series of protests were organised across Northern Ireland (some of which turned violent) and a number of riots occurred. Five deaths resulted from the street violence, and the protests ultimately proved to be counterproductive – achieving little apart from alienating many of the public and LAW's own members.

By late 1973, after a period of in-fighting, leadership struggles and accusations of theft of group funds, LAW was a spent political movement, undermined by internal conflicting interests and the absence of a coherent political strategy. Billy withdrew from workers' politics and, in January 1974, LAW was replaced by the Ulster Workers' Council – a more articulate, better-led organisation which had a looser association with loyalist paramilitary groupings than its predecessor.

In early 1974 Hull was in a glazier's shop on the Crumlin Road with James Anderson, the shop's owner and acting chairman of the UDA. Two armed men burst in and fired several rounds at Anderson and Hull before escaping. Anderson was injured but survived. Hull only escaped injury (or worse), when a bullet intended to kill embedded itself in a large pocket-watch he wore under his jacket. For months afterwards he proudly exhibited to friends the lifesaving watch with its tell-tale indent.

Meanwhile, back in the shipyard where it had all begun, Billy Hull had transferred his talents to once again resolving industrial disputes. From typical decent working-class stock, he had found himself out of his depth in the mire of Ulster politics – and almost paid with his life.

The remainder of his shipyard and political career was lived out in relative obscurity. But the James Young caricature, Billy Hulk, haunted him for a long time.

# CECIL

Cecil was one of the many shipyard workers who found a way to wander around the shipyard unchallenged. His actual job in the Yard was never entirely clear, but few ever questioned him, as he was such a decent, likeable character. He would appear in the Joiners' Shop several times a week, often carrying mysterious folders under the arm. He was popular and, when the Gaffer wasn't around, he stopped for a chat, regaling anyone who would listen with an endless flow of interesting stories and shipyard gossip.

His visits were always welcome not least because he was always willing to 'run a message' for anyone who needed a packet of cigarettes from Harlands' underground enterprises, or who wanted to place a bet at one of the numerous illegal bookies. All this he did without seeking payment or favour.

But Cecil had one disarming disability which no one, out of respect for him, corrected or challenged – his grasp of the nuances of the English language could, on occasion, be confusing (to put it kindly). On one of his visits to the Joiners' Shop, he was in an unusually grim mood as he spoke to one of his regulars. 'I had to take the cat to the vet yesterday. It was up all night, as sick as a dog. He charged me nearly twice the same as last time. When I queried the bill, he made the excuse it wasn't his fault but was due to rising infatuation.'

This wasn't Cecil's first visit to the vet either. Months earlier he had been concerned about the number of kittens his pet was producing and was experiencing difficulty in finding good homes for them. While the common practice then was to place unwanted kittens in a bucket of water and weigh them down with lumps of coal until they drowned, Cecil could never bring himself to carry out such a barbaric ritual. He was therefore overjoyed to learn that there was a more humane way to stop the unwanted litters. 'I took it to the vet for advice. He charged me a pound and good value it was too. The cat can't have any more kittens because it's been incarcerated.'

Another day he described his wife's uncle's funeral. 'Ninety-four he was when he died, in perfect health until the last breath – and him still with all his facilities. He never smoked or drunk. The undertaker said he never saw a healthier corpse. That may be, but the uncle was a miserable old bugger. By the way could you lend me five Woodbines until Friday?' And no one ever refused Cecil's requests, or asked for repayment.

In a conversation with another joiner he related the trauma of the time when the British currency became decimal. 'One day I went into a strange shop to purchase cigarettes. I emptied my pockets of the new money and said to the woman behind the counter, "There you are, missus. Take what you want and give me ten Park Drive. I haven't got the hang of this new dismal money yet." She scooped up the lot – no change, and said I was lucky, there was just enough. I reckon that oul' doll done me in my money. Anyhow, I never frequanted that shop again.'

Cecil was also an authority on royal protocol, or at least he thought he was. In 1953, during the period of public debate following the news that Princess Margaret intended to marry the divorced RAF officer Peter Townsend, Cecil explained the legal position – if Margaret married a divorced man, she would be 'excommunicated' by the Queen.

His grasp on religious matters was even more tenuous.

'I can't see all these economical discussions between church leaders making any progress. As long as Catholics insist the Pope is inflammable, they're just wasting their time.'

# THE SAWMILL

In the 1960s there was a 'runner' at Harlands called Sydney McKibbin – a courier whose main territory included the Alexander Works. He was ideally placed to collect tittle-tattle throughout the day from his everyday contacts, so when Sydney found a willing audience during his official duties, his opening gambit was, invariably, 'You're never going to believe this.' And without waiting for a response, he would then launch into yet another dramatic story, or the latest gossip (which was usually garbled). Some of the workers suspected that the information fed to him was deliberately fictitious in order to test his credulity as well as fool his listeners. But Sydney, unsophisticated and trusting, had no such misgivings.

One day more excitable than usual and hardly able to contain himself, he cornered a joiner friend. 'I was talking to a labourer at the Logs today.' (The Logs was the open area behind the Joiners' Shop where the raw timber was stored before being taken to the nearby sawmill. It was also the place where apprentice joiners would go at lunchtime to resolve any disputes. Many a black eye appeared in the afternoon that had not been apparent that morning.) 'You're not going to believe what I've heard about the strange goings-on in the sawmill,' said Sydney. His informant, he claimed, had related a series of bizarre incidents that had apparently occurred over the past year and asked him to keep it confidential in case news of the events reached the ears of the management. Asking Sydney to keep something secret was akin to submitting your story to the *News of The World*.

According to Sydney's contact, one of the machinists in the sawmill had accidentally lost a hand under a large log-cutting saw. A quick-thinking supervisor took immediate action and obtained a plastic bag packed with ice from the shipyard canteen next door. He wrapped the severed hand in ice, and rushed it and the injured man to the Ulster Hospital. A successful transplant was carried out and within a month the man had full use of his hand and had returned to work. The only after-effect was a welcome compensation cheque for £5,000.

Another machinist, learning of the incident, was alerted to the potential to earn a useful lump sum. He reasoned that a more serious accident would attract a higher level of compensation than £5,000, so the next day he 'accidentally' tripped after running a log through the powered saw. His arm ran across the path of the saw and was severed above the elbow. His screams attracted the attention of the Gaffer who once again took rapid action – a plastic bag was packed with ice from the canteen and the arm was carefully wrapped up. The workman was transported immediately to the Ulster Hospital. The subsequent transplant of the injured arm was a miraculous piece of corrective surgery, and within a month he was back at work in the sawmill with no evidence of the ordeal and a fully functioning arm. Soon after, his solicitor advised him that there would be compensation of £18,000.

A fellow sawyer had been following the accident proceedings with keen interest. His mathematical competence was usually confined to calculating the returns on a complicated 'treble' or an 'each-way double-lap' gamble at the bookies. Working out the benefits of a sawmill accident posed little challenge for him. £5,000 compensation for a hand injury, £18,000 for an arm – a more serious mishap would guarantee a considerably higher payment! The logic was impeccable. But an accident more drastic and ambitious than the others was necessary. He had a brainwave. At the first opportunity he put it into action.

One day when no one was watching, he lay over the saw bench. The massive whirring sawblade bore down and neatly sliced off his head like a knife through butter. As it rolled away into the sawdust, a horrified workmate raised the alarm, bringing the Gaffer to the scene. The well-practised emergency drill sprung into action – the head was gently gathered up and placed in a plastic bag full of ice. The head and the workman were quickly removed by ambulance to the hospital.

That evening the workman's wife visited the Ulster Hospital to check on his condition. She was met by a senior surgeon. He informed her that her husband was dead. 'You can't be serious,' she said. 'Why didn't you reconnect him like you did with the other accidents?' 'I tried to,' explained the surgeon, 'but unfortunately, some idiot put the head in a plastic bag and your husband suffocated.'

As he related the story Sydney McKibbin became agitated. 'Would you believe that anyone could be so stupid? Sure every bugger knows that plastic bags are dangerous.'

# MARGE OR BUTTER

During the days of Per Nielsen's appointment as Deputy Chief Executive, a persistent story circulated that appears to have substance in fact. On a tour of the Harland complex one day he noticed a man standing outside a workshop, smoking during working hours.

He challenged the man, 'Do you know who I am?'

'Not at all,' came the reply.

Nielsen then asked, 'Can you tell margarine from butter?'

'Sure I can. Why?' said the puzzled worker.

'That's good news,' snapped Nielsen. 'That's all you'll be getting next week. You're sacked. Pick up your cards on Friday!'

# THE DIESEL GENIUS

Edward Harland, Gustav Wolff, Sir Frederick Rebbeck, Lord Pirrie, Thomas Andrews and others who controlled Harland & Wolff during its prosperous years, have indelibly stamped their personalities on the public perception of the Belfast shipyard. Their names and unique contributions in making Harlands the most successful shipbuilders in the world, are recognised and enshrined in the company's history.

But one influential person whose name is often missing from that elite list of progressive shipyard directors is Cuthbert Coulson Pounder. The rare name Pounder may trigger faint recall of the one-time south Belfast Unionist MP, Rafton Pounder, C.C.'s son. But who was C.C. Pounder? Few of the yard's thousands of workers who benefited from his genius or, the wider general public, were aware of the vital part he played in the shipyard's success.

As a 'back room genius', his name became a byword for brilliance in the marine engines world both in the UK and internationally. Pounder's contribution to Harlands' reputation also was immeasurable. Born in 1891, he served an engineering apprenticeship with a Hartlepool company. At twenty-five years of age he moved to Harland & Wolff, and Ulster was his home for the rest of his long life. His career at the Queen's Island brought rapid promotion and he eventually became Chief Engineer and Technical Director at the company. During his working life he was responsible for the design of 1,200 propulsion systems of all types (steam and diesel) that aggregated an astonishing six million horse-power. And by the age of thirty, he had written two textbooks on marine engineering. These became recommended reading for young aspiring engineers. Although mainly associated with diesel engine development, he also pioneered progress on steam engines.

As well as being a skilled, innovative engineer, Pounder had a philosophical mind. 'Engines', he said, 'are hard taskmasters. Lose or win, kill or cure, heaven or hell, the doctor, the lawyer, the cleric may receive their fees, but when things go wrong with the machine, the engineer's competence is quickly called into question.' However, as an acknowledged expert in his field, Pounder was more than competent. One technical writer on the subject of motor shipping recorded, 'men of this calibre believed in the motor ship and believed that Northern Ireland could build a better motor ship than any other place in the world. As well as being in the vanguard of marine diesel engine development, they are equally well able to build many other types of engines. These men are not without a sense of humour; they know their shipowners as any salesman; they are psychologists as well as engineers.'

Pounder's skills and confidence were put to the test in the 1930s when the Union-Castle Mail Steamship Company commissioned the construction of two liners, on the condition that Harlands could supply 32,000-horsepower diesel engines – greater than any other engine afloat. It was a nail-biting challenge for Harlands to design and build from scratch an engine of unprecedented power, and Pounder was asked to give an assurance that the design was achievable. Failure would have resulted in bankruptcy for the yard. Pounder met the challenge unflinchingly. His reaction was born of his philosophy: 'Achievement was always a story of burned boats, of taking hazards born of knowledge and conviction, always with one's future and reputation as the stake.' The new machinery was designed in time and the two 25,500-ton passenger ships, *Stirling Castle* and *Athlone Castle*, were delivered to the owners in 1936, resulting in substantial profits for Harland & Wolff.

A few years later Pounder had to accept responsibility for designing and building six prototype engines that would go straight from the drawing board to installation on the ships. Never before had the process of prolonged test-bed trials of prototypes been bypassed, but the real test bed, Pounder claimed, was the high seas! The prototypes were a resounding success.

Over many years, under Pounder's inspiration and talents, the volume and value of continuous development of marine engines at Belfast had no equivalent anywhere in Britain. The massive Engine Works on the Queens Road and the monster machinery produced there were testimony to the workmanship and world demand for innovative and reliable engines of various types.

Some of the great passenger liners with which Pounder is associated include the *Andes*, the *Predennis Castle* and the *Southern Cross*. He wrote extensively on marine engineering topics and for fourteen years he was vice-president of the Institute of Marine Engineers, becoming president in 1961. He devoted considerable time to the affairs of many engineering institutions, including the Royal Institution of Naval Architects. He was the recipient of many awards for outstanding services to engineering.

Once, when he was asked what the most important achievement of his career had been, he replied that it was not the successful mastery of the many problems associated with the development of prime movers, it was any part he might have played in breaking down antagonisms between competitive firms and establishing goodwill to the benefit of all, including his own workers.

A strict taskmaster who did not suffer fools gladly, he retired in 1965 after forty-nine years of service with Harland & Wolff. His career spanned a tumultuous period that included the traumatic *Titanic* disaster, several recessions and two world wars – all of which brought fresh difficulties to the Belfast yard. A pressing challenge of those times was how to adapt technically and commercially – but with a superbly innovative, internationally acclaimed engineer such as C.C. Pounder in charge, the design and production of marine engines kept the Queen's Island at the forefront of world shipbuilding.

Pounder, who did not mince words, in later years expressed the view that there were three 'P' words in the English language that he intensely disliked – prestige, precedent and priest. He disliked them all for the same reason, namely they were, he said, 'pungent with humbug'. Another time when he was asked for his reflection on life in general, he replied, 'Would that we were endowed with foresight as we are with hindsight. We'd be better off with damnsight.'

With his avowed dislike of prestige, it seems fitting that Pounder received the anonymity that he might have preferred, but his achievements – when measured against other higher-profile shipyard personalities – suggest that his long, outstanding service to shipbuilding in general, and Belfast in particular, still justified greater recognition in his lifetime.

C.C. Pounder died on 20 December 1982 at his home near Drumbo, County Down. He was ninety-one years old.

# THE MUSIC MAKERS

Northern Ireland has long enjoyed a thriving music culture. Performers such as Hamilton Harty, James Galway, Van Morrison, Barry Douglas, James Johnston (the opera-singing butcher from Sandy Row), the Ulster Orchestra, Snow Patrol and many others, had their genesis in Ulster. That wide category of music makers also includes several choirs and choral groups, founded in churches or schools that later moved into a wider public arena.

Some well-known Ulster choirs, however, had a more unorthodox beginning. Visualise a shipyard riveter standing on a narrow staging plank, precariously balanced 100 feet above ground, inches from possible death. He is dirty, sweating and wielding a heavy pneumatic machine which, along with nearby machines, is generating a deafening din. His colleagues across the shipyard are working under the same noisy, body-racking conditions – a more unlikely environment for the emergence of musical expression would be difficult to imagine. Yet from the industrial backdrop of Queen's Island, not one but three outstanding choirs emerged and in time achieved critical acclaim and popular support.

The first two choirs were formed in the 1910s. In 1912 the Queen's Island Choir, the oldest in Ulster, was formed at Harland & Wolff; and in 1916 – possibly as a response to the cultural initiative of their shipbuilding neighbours – the workers at Workman Clark's Victoria Yard and Works formed the Victoria Choir.

From earliest times the choirs performed to increasingly appreciative audiences, locally and in Britain. During the difficult years of recession and frequent pre-war lay-offs, the choirs served an important social role in maintaining friendships among workers and generated optimism that a better future lay ahead. In 1935, when Workman Clark went bankrupt and Harlands bought the Victoria Yard and Works, the two choirs remained, retaining their independence.

Throughout the Second World War, the choirs performed with great success in festivals across the United Kingdom, and in April 1941, after the devastating Blitz on Harland & Wolff, the Queen's Island Choir made various national broadcasts on the BBC, probably organised in part as propaganda to convince the enemy that shipbuilding production in Belfast had largely escaped serious disruption.

With restricted travel between Britain and Ireland during the war, very few cross-channel artists were able to perform in Ulster. Most live entertainment was provided by local talent – of which there was no dearth. Part of that demand was met by the shipyard choirs who enjoyed pre-eminence among their peers.

In 1944 another choir was established. One day in November a group of workers were singing around a coke fire in the Victoria Works during a lunch break. The daily sing-songs had become a regular feature. Someone – impressed by the quality and repertoire of the singers – suggested, 'Why not form a proper choir?' A meeting was called to find out how many men would be interested, and the response was so overwhelming that rehearsals were organised straight away. As some of the choir members worked long shifts, rehearsals were not possible outside normal working hours so Harlands management made a large air raid shelter available for practice during lunchtimes. A conductor was appointed from within the members, and the Harlandic Male Voice Choir was formed.

From these modest beginnings, the choir made good progress and, in a fairly short time, outgrew its shipyard facilities. In 1945 they hired a hall in Belfast city centre and appointed the choir's first full-time musical director. Under professional guidance, the choir developed rapidly and enjoyed a growing enthusiastic membership. Members would often attend rehearsals direct from work still wearing boiler suits and overalls. A major landmark in the choir's progress was entering and winning the Larne Competitive Music Festival in the late 1940s with a high average scoring of 92 points. That was the first of many awards.

The Harlandic Male Voice Choir has won the BBC 'Let the People Sing' competition a record-breaking four times and represented the UK in the European finals of the competition three times. The choir has participated in many radio and TV broadcasts, both locally and nationally, as well as performing in many cathedrals and churches. A successful sixteen-day tour of Canada and the USA took place in 1998.

The original enthusiasm and interest levels show no signs of abating, but while membership originally had been limited to Harland & Wolff workers, it is now open to the wider community. The continuing nationwide reputation and success of the Harlandic is a resounding vindication of the confidence of the shipyard workers who practised in a damp air raid shelter during the dark days of the war in 1944.

The three shipyard choirs, the Harlandic Male Voice Choir, the Queen's Island Choir and the Victoria Choir, co-existed for about thirty years, each enjoying the support of a loyal fan base across the province. But with the onset of the Troubles in 1969, the entire social fabric of Northern Ireland began to disintegrate. People were reluctant to leave their homes at night, particularly around Belfast, so night life and entertainment of all types suffered through lack of public support. With diminishing membership and fewer bookings, the Queen's Island and the Victoria Choirs were forced to merge in 1974 in order to survive. Renamed the Queen's Island Victoria Choir it managed to re-establish itself and emerged from the Troubles a little slimmer, but still performing with the panache that had delighted earlier audiences. Since then it continues to go from strength to strength. Among its successes are several appearances with the Welsh Association of Male Choirs at the Royal Albert Hall, a performance with the Haverfordwest Male Choir and their special guest artiste Aled Jones, and singing with the QIVMC and Warringtown Primary School Choir, winners of the junior section of Songs of Praise Choir for 2004.

From a reformed choir that struggled to survive the traumatic decades of Ulster's political upheaval, the Queen's Island Victoria Choir continues to entertain audiences across Northern Ireland and elsewhere, and retains the tradition and reputation established by its former members almost a century earlier.

Belfast today boasts two excellent choirs that have strong traditional associations with Queen's Island. Shipbuilding may be only a memory, but the musical entertainment performed by the choirs under their present famous titles is a fitting and evocative reminder of their pedigree and origins.

# THE YARD PLAYWRIGHTS

The development of successful shipyard choirs might be considered unlikely in an industrial environment such as shipbuilding. However, the same working conditions also inspired other Islandmen to express their talents and experiences in a different art form – as playwrights. The achievements of three workers in particular, Thomas Carnduff, Sam Thompson and Wilson John Haire – one a steel worker, one a painter and one a joiner – are remarkable. Largely self-taught, they used everyday events as a way to examine larger social and political issues. In some cases, they showed their audiences the secret and fascinating world of the shipyards.

That the Belfast shipyard environment, which mainly recruited its labour force from men of working-class stock with only basic educational attainments, could inspire and spawn men of the stature of Carnduff, Thompson, Haire and others, is an outstanding tribute to a world-famous industry more noted for building magnificent ships. Perhaps it also suggests that grand human achievements are independent of external influences. If talent and burning passions exist, they can overcome most obstacles.

## Thomas Carnduff – The Shipyard Poet

Visitors to the Linenhall Library, Belfast, in the 1950s probably paid scant attention to the resident caretaker – an elderly figure who quietly went about his duties. Few, apart from the literary fraternity, would have recognised Thomas Carnduff, better known as the 'Shipyard Poet' or sometimes the 'People's Poet'.

In his lifetime, his prolific outpouring of poetry, plays and contemporary prose reflected a passion for the city of his birth and a social reformer's zeal to advance the economic and social status of its working-class citizens.

Carnduff, himself of solid working-class stock, was born in Kensington Street, Sandy Row, in 1886. In common with most of his generation, on leaving school at fourteen, his teenage years were spent in various menial jobs, working, amongst other things, as a butcher's boy, factory hand and Catch Boy in a Belfast shipyard – all hard work for poor pay. From 1906–14 he worked as an assistant in the stereotyping section of the Belfast Steam Print Company, where he revelled in the camaraderie of his well-versed, articulate co-workers. He read widely in order to contribute to their stimulating levels of daily debate on the social issues of the time.

Following the outbreak of war in 1914, Carnduff spent two years as a driller in the Workman Clark shipyard on the Lagan. In 1916 he enlisted in the Royal Engineers and served at Ypres and Messines. On demob from the army in 1919, he was re-employed at Workmans as a plater's helper at a rate of twenty-one shillings (£1.05) for a fifty-four hour week – working from 6 a.m. to 5.30 p.m every day. It was arduous, dangerous labour which often involved working at heights – the fear of which Carnduff never entirely overcame in his long shipbuilding career. Accidents were a daily occurrence in the yard, and on one occasion, Carnduff was taken to hospital after suffering injuries from a heavy spanner dropped from 40 feet.

As a youth Carnduff had written poetry – experimenting with what he called 'doggerel' – and during his early days in the shipyard he was inspired to write about his experiences there. A collection of writings, called *Songs from the Shipyard and other Poems*, was published in 1924 and dedicated to, 'My comrades of the shipyards and of the days and nights toil we spent together'. The book, funded by a sympathetic relative, captured the rich vein of social and human activity in which he now played a part but, unfortunately, it did not sell well – it was a huge disappointment to Carnduff and his sponsor.

The unsuccessful publication of *Songs of the Shipyard* corresponded with a year-long lay off from the shipyard. Indeed, his seventeen years of employment with Workman Clark, in common with many others, would be punctuated by regular lay offs. Occasional poems and articles in Belfast and Dublin newspapers earned pittances, and did little to relieve the hardships of feeding and supporting his family of six. A dole allowance of twenty-seven shillings (£1.35), which was only paid four weeks in five, hardly reduced the poverty and sense of despair. As time passed and Carnduff was still without a job – because there were no jobs! – even those payments stopped.

After a brief foray into self-employment, typing plays, sermons and poetry for others, he was encouraged by Ulster writer Richard Rowley to write a play. Choosing to write about his experiences in the shipyards, Carnduff produced *Workers*. Several attempts to have the play performed locally were unsuccessful, but in 1932 it opened at Dublin's Abbey Theatre. Carnduff recalled his anticipation of the performance. 'The pleasure of seeing one's efforts in a public theatre, and one with an international fame, when the author is an unemployed shipyard man, is an episode incapable of recording.' The authentic portrayal of life in a Northern shipyard, acted with unfamiliar Belfast accents, enhanced the play's appeal. Later, as he took rapturous curtain calls: 'An unholy joy took possession of me. Years of poverty, misery, disappointment were forgotten in that solitary moment.'

Following the success of the Dublin premiere, *Workers* played at the Empire Theatre, Belfast, to equally enthusiastic audiences. The applause of Carnduff's former workmates packing the 'gods' was music to his ears.

In 1935 he was laid off for the last time from Workman Clark when the shipyard went bankrupt and closed. But the success of *Workers* had led to commissions for plays and poetry, as well as invitations to lecture on drama and social issues. He would go on to write plays such as *Machinery, Traitors* and *Castlereagh*, deriving inspiration from his on-off working days in Workman Clark's shipyard, and the history and environment of a much-loved Belfast.

Thomas Carnduff died on 16 April 1956, but he left behind a legacy of exceptional writing and social commentary. He had used his writings to highlight the plight of the under-privileged and to inspire them to realise their higher potential. He strove to demonstrate that the working classes merited a valued place in modern society.

While other better-off, tutored classes scorned or simply ignored what appeared to them a coarse, unlettered daily army of Islandmen in boiler suits and duncher headgear, he had a more intimate, sympathetic perspective on his fellow workers. His vision of them was that of a hard-working, compassionate community dedicated to an onerous occupation, who took fierce pride in their achievements. Thanks to their skills, mountains of rusting steel plates and other materials were transformed into magnificent ocean-going liners that travelled the world – luxury voyages which the builders themselves would never experience.

*

## Sam Thompson

On 26 January 1960, in a struggling Belfast theatre, a bomb-shell of a play was performed – one that would shatter for all time the cosy, elitist world of serious Ulster drama. The performance ran for six weeks to full houses, and was a huge success for its author and producers.

The play, *Over the Bridge*, by Harland & Wolff painter Sam Thompson, raised profound questions about religious tensions and prejudices within Northern Ireland society and, in tackling such a taboo subject, it challenged local theatrical tradition which tended to steer clear of such controversial matters.

*Over the Bridge* was based on shipyard incidents of the 1930s and was performed during the ongoing IRA campaign of 1956–61. For some, Thompson's play was an overdue exposure of sectarian prejudices against Catholics; others disagreed vehemently. Many were also shocked by the coarseness of the dialogue and the passion exhibited in public, albeit on a stage. If the author had intended to stimulate discussion about Ulster political attitudes, he certainly achieved his objectives, and more.

Sam Thompson, born in 1916, was the seventh in a family of eight children, born and raised in Montrose Street, off Newtownards Road, Belfast. His father, a lamplighter with the City Corporation, eked out his meagre wages with a part-time sexton's job at the nearby St Clement's Church. When Sam entered Harland & Wolff in 1932 as apprentice painter, he was concerned that, like his brother, he would be sacked as soon as he served his time. At the time shipbuilding nationwide was at its lowest ebb – there were few orders, empty slipways and thousands out of work.

Thompson recalled that, when a few vacancies were

heard of through the grapevine, hundreds of starving, ragged men would cluster around the shipyard gates hoping for work. Anxious men would push and manhandle each other to find a better position and hopefully draw a foreman's favourable attention. When the quota had been filled, some still hung around in futile hope long after he had gone. Others departed, often in tears, to go back to their homes and starving families. Scenes like that, witnessed in Thompson's youth, burned into his psyche the injustices and suffering of the labouring classes.

He became a member of the Painter's Union, and eventually a shop steward, and there he found a platform where he could campaign for social reform. Regular meetings of interested workers took place in the shipyard toilets to debate the urgent issues of the day and to discuss possible means of resolving them. The meetings embraced a wide range of opinions and sometimes ended in violence as extreme views were exchanged. But Thompson grew impatient at the slow political progress made in the shipyard, and decided to leave his native Belfast.

He left for Manchester, believing it to have more promising opportunities, and worked there for six years but in 1945 he returned to Belfast. Although work was available at Harland & Wolff, he chose self-employment instead, and started a decorating business. The enterprise was unsuccessful and he was forced to seek work with the Belfast Corporation. As an employee once again, he inevitably became involved in trade union activities and was elected as shop steward. It was claimed that his later sacking from the Corporation was due to his over-zealous union activities. But his absence from the shipyard and its mass workforce denied him a wide enough platform to discuss and progress social matters. That vacuum was filled when he moved from

Newtownards Road to Craigmore Street, off Ormeau Avenue, Belfast.

The nearby Elbow Room pub on the Dublin Road was the focal point for an extraordinary cross section of Belfast clientele. Apart from the everyday pint shifters, it was frequented by actors, journalists, BBC staff and others who had come to do business, or to join in the regular debates on a wide range of issues – it was an introduction to a new layer of Belfast society for Thompson. His first tentative steps into the theatrical world were inspired by friendships made at that pub and he was soon obtaining minor acting and directing roles with the Rosemary Players and other amateur societies. Other acting parts in the Group Theatre followed.

After an encounter with Sam Hanna Bell, a progressive BBC producer, Thompson began writing for radio, producing shows such as *A Brush in Hand*, about an apprentice shipyard painter, a documentary, *Tommy Baxter, Shop Steward*, and a weekly serial, *The Fairmans*.

Apart from his now busy writing career, Thompson was volubly promoting the ideals of socialism and had become an active member of the Northern Ireland Labour Party (NILP) which, in the mid-1950s, was beginning to make serious inroads into the traditional Belfast Unionist vote. Paddy Devlin, an NILP member and later founder member of the SDLP, described a meeting he had with Thompson. 'I liked him instantly. He was an uncomplicated straight shooter who always appeared to be smouldering on the edge of explosion into flames at the sight and sound of injustice. Everyone within earshot knew where Sam stood on every issue. If they did not, it never took Sam long to tell them.'

Thompson meanwhile, ever the ardent socialist, had ambitions of more substantial writing than documentaries or stories for radio audiences – he had an overwhelming desire to expose some of the sectarianism he had seen or heard about in the shipyard. I didn't witness any incidents of prejudice or discrimination during my own time at Harlands – the religion of others was not important to me, and relationships with fellow workers were based on a man's personality and our interactions. But while matters had improved somewhat since the Second World War, there was still a deeply ingrained sectarianism present in the shipyards, and Thompson was determined to throw a spotlight on it. In 1958, after two years of intensive writing, he completed what became his seminal, dramatic work, *Over the Bridge*. The 'bridge' in question was a matter of debate. Was it the Queen's Bridge over the Lagan, or Fraser Street Bridge, off Newtownards Road, which led directly into the shipyard?

At the time, actor James Ellis was artistic director of the Group Theatre, Belfast. He was always keen to promote fresh local writing talent, so when Sam Thompson approached him with the challenge, 'I've got a play you wouldn't touch with a barge pole,' Ellis was intrigued. He took on the challenge, knowing that the play would be controversial.

However, two weeks before the public performance, the Group's board Chairman, Ritchie McKee, requested substantial cuts to the script. He informed the *Belfast Telegraph*: 'The play is full of grossly vicious phrases and situations which would offend every section of the public. It is the policy of the Ulster Group Theatre to keep political and religious controversies off our stage.'

Ellis and Thompson refused to meet McKee's request to cut the text, and they, along with other prominent Group actors, resigned. They formed their own theatre group, Ulster Bridge Productions and eventually found an alternative venue. The Empire Theatre in Belfast was spacious and opulent, and was a high-risk, expensive venue to launch a controversial drama. But the confidence of Ellis and Thompson was vindicated. *Over the Bridge*, played with a well-known Ulster cast (including Thompson in a minor role), was a resounding overnight success. Audiences of forty-two thousand attended its six-week run – a record for a play performed in Belfast. The profitable Belfast premiere was followed by performances in Dublin, Glasgow, Edinburgh and Brighton. A run in London, not surprisingly, was less successful. The play was later adapted for TV by Granada Television and BBC radio. As expected, reaction in Thompson's home city was mixed. Many were shocked by the crude language and implied brutality on the stage. Others saw it as an attack on or distortion of their religious and political beliefs. To others it was a vindication of their long-held grievances.

The success of *Over the Bridge* launched Thompson into a relentless, bruising writing routine, and three other plays followed. *The Evangelist*, about the nineteenth-century religious revival in Ireland, was successfully played in the Opera House, Belfast, in 1963. *Cemented with Love*, which had a theme of political corruption, was intended for broadcast in 1964, but was postponed due to a pending election. It was eventually performed in May 1965. Sadly, Thompson did not see it. He had died on 15 February 1965 from a heart attack. His last play, *Masquerade*, still in draft stage and set in London, was never completed or performed.

Sam Thompson's passing at the early age of forty-nine was a serious loss to Ulster's theatrical society as well as to Belfast's close-knit socialist fraternity which was in need of popular figures to promote its cause. His death was also a devastating shock to his numerous personal friends who had shared his failures and triumphs over many years. Probably most traumatic was the loss to his wife, May, who witnessed at first hand, the struggles, disappointments as well as family sacrifices this self-taught playwright and former shipyard worker had endured in his efforts to change an unfair world.

## Wilson John Haire

Haire's early background, neither urban nor industrial, was vastly different to the other shipyard writers. He was born in 1932 on the Shankill Road, Belfast. His mother, a Roman Catholic, came from a landowning family in Omagh, County Tyrone, while his father, a Presbyterian, was a tradesman joiner. When Haire was still young, his family moved to Carryduff, County Down – a rural setting that was still a reasonable distance from Belfast, where most available jobs were located.

The five Haire children – Wilson and his four sisters – were enrolled as Roman Catholics in the local Clontoncally Public Elementary School. It was a state school where provision was made for Catholic pupils to start late in the morning so that they would miss the Presbyterian assembly. Haire's recorded memories of early life in Carryduff are vague – his writings take the format of biographical fiction. But it does appear that, despite the difficult economic climate of the 1930s, hardship was not a feature of life in the Haire family, although poverty was widespread in their local community.

Wilson, against his parents' wishes, left school at fourteen years of age to obtain a job as office boy at Harland & Wolff. The transition from a rural way of life to the heavily industrialised world of shipbuilding must have been an emotional and cultural shock for young Haire.

Two years later, he paid his five pounds deposit – a hefty sum in those days – and became an indentured apprentice joiner. He was a colleague of mine in the Joiners' Shop and his memories of that period – when fact and fiction can be separated – are recorded in his book, *The Yard*, which describes a way of working life now long gone. The shipyard stories, characters and working conditions have a ring of authenticity, but his use of fictional characters and situations will upset sticklers for historical accuracy.

On completion of his five-year apprenticeship in the cavernous Joiners' Shop – in which his father had also worked during the war years when it was used for building Stirling bomber fuselages – Haire became restless. He wanted a change from the constraints of his family life and his work routine. He had just begun to earn full wages as a tradesman, but he handed in his board for the last time and resigned from Harland & Wolff, despite having no other job to go to. It was a typically impetuous act which undoubtedly earned his parents disapproval.

However, he soon secured another job – that of Ballroom Supervisor in the vast Plaza dance hall in Chichester Street, Belfast, the largest such hall in Northern Ireland. Haire, in his tuxedo and bow tie, maintained public order on dance nights – a role far removed from his earlier career as a one-among-many white-aproned joiner. He now enjoyed authority and style.

At only twenty-two years of age, he became impatient for change and fresh challenges once again. As a trained joiner – at a time when a joiner, especially a shipyard one, was considered to be one of the elite, and more skilled than a regular carpenter – Haire had no difficulty obtaining a carpenter's job in London. Around 1960, after several years in London, a disposition towards and latent talent for writing began to emerge.

Three stories, 'Refuge from the Tickman', 'The Beg',

and 'The Screening' were published in the *Irish Democrat*, a London weekly newspaper. A subsequent foray into drama writing produced two one-act plays – *The Clockwork Orange*, centred around a controversial Belfast protest by the Reverend Ian Paisley; and *Divil Era*, about the B-Specials – both of which were performed and well-received at Hampstead Theatre, London. It was an encouraging start to a career in dramatic theatre for a novice playwright with no previous history in or predisposition toward the performing arts.

Although he lived for a relatively short time in his native Ulster, his early writings are coloured by a Catholic perspective, and most of his dramatic output was inspired by the political and religious complexities of life in Northern Ireland. In his later career – as indicated by plays such as *Lost Worlds*, performed at the Academy of Dramatic Art, London, in 1984 – he has moved away from exploring Ulster's political themes, and instead covers the wider global arena of social justice.

He has received drama awards from various British arts councils and theatres, and in 1974, the *London Evening Standard* acclaimed him as 'the most outstanding playwright'. In recognition of his commercial and artistic success, he became resident dramatist at the Royal Court Theatre, London. A year later, he spent a brief period in Belfast as resident dramatist at the Lyric.

Apart from his prolific playwriting career, he has written numerous articles on socialist issues, which have been published in various labour and trade unions publications. He has also written over a dozen poems on socialist and secular subjects which have been widely distributed.

Regrettably his national (and, later, international) recognition as a serious playwright has not been matched by similar acclaim in his native country, where he remains largely unknown. Though this may be partly his own fault. Unlike Thomas Carnduff and Sam Thompson, who unashamedly displayed a passion and affection for their birthplace, Haire's works seem to portray only the negative aspects of his homeland, and, since he left Northern Ireland for good, there has been little evidence of any deep affinity or affection for it.

Haire's considerable creativity and energy have recently been used to explore and influence important and much wider global issues. This is not out of character. It was evident when he walked out of the Belfast shipyard, served only a short time as a dancehall bouncer, became a London carpenter and took up writing, that he was willing to challenge the status quo. Such restlessness and willingness to face new challenges are refreshing in a world where a sense of security is more attractive than taking risks. Individuals such as Haire are often the catalyst that eventually changes society.

# SHIPYARD ROOTS

The shipyards of Belfast have produced their fair share of famous faces over the years. Some of the more ambitious workers – who may have begun their working lives as joiners, electricians, metal workers, or any of the other hundreds of trades present in the yards – left the security of Queen's Island to seek alternative careers – perhaps as footballers, playwrights, musicians or politicians.

But there were also those who, while they may not have worked directly in or for the shipyards, benefited from the experience, the wisdom, and the tutelage of the Auld Hands ...

## *Van Morrison*

George Morrison was a Harland & Wolff electrician in the 1950s – only one of the many who worked on the Queen's Island. What marked him out from his fellow tradesmen was his obsession with collecting ten-inch 78 records. Not for him the latest popular releases being sold in the Smithfield market stalls (Frankie Laine, Guy Mitchell and others): Morrison's musical tastes were much more specialised and eclectic. He preferred American artists and his choices embraced a wide genre of musical styles – rhythm and blues, country gospel, jazz, soul, and the more recent skiffle. It was reputed that he had one of the largest private record collections in Ulster.

The music of American legends such as Lead Belly, Muddy Waters, Ray Charles, Solomon Burke and countless others filled his small terraced home in Hyndford Street, east Belfast, and this love of music was passed along to his son, Ivan Morrison – better known to the world as acclaimed singer-songwriter, Van Morrison.

'Van the Man' (as he's known to his fans) has produced hits like 'Brown Eyed Girl' and 'Bright Side of the Road', and critically acclaimed albums such as *Astral Weeks* and *Moondance*. He has toured all over the world, received numerous awards and accolades (including induction into the Rock and Roll Hall of Fame), and even received an OBE. But it was growing up with that 'different' style of music playing in his home that was the inspiration that carried him into the top echelon of world-famous entertainers. As he confessed in one of his rare media interviews, 'If it weren't for guys like Ray and Solomon, I wouldn't be where I am today. Those guys were the inspiration that got me going. If it wasn't for that kind of music, I couldn't do what I'm doing now.'

It is unlikely that an ordinary shipyard worker like George Morrison would have have fantasised that his rare record collection would one day inspire and launch his son Ivan into a career that would reach across continents, and make him into an internationally renowned musical phenomenon – or that the modest terraced house at 125 Hyndford Street, Belfast, where it all began, would become a tourist destination and pilgrimage dream for many of Van Morrison's loyal supporters. But there can be no doubt that Van has placed Belfast on the entertainment map of the world, and that this is, in no small part, thanks to a Harland & Wolff electrician, earning eleven pounds a week, who had a passion for collecting off-beat 78 records!

*

## James Galway

James Galway, born 1939, is an internationally renowned flautist, who has performed with the world's leading orchestras and conductors, and has gained for himself the well-merited title 'virtuoso'. His version of 'Annie's Song' (originally by John Denver) became hugely successful in the popular music market, introducing him to thousands of new fans for his brand of music which today embraces classical, jazz, folk and other styles, all given a unique 'Galway' interpretation which delights audiences worldwide. His album sales have earned him several platinum and gold record awards.

In recognition of his services to music, Galway was awarded an OBE in 1979 and in 2001 he was knighted. 'The Man with the Golden Flute' continues to perform internationally before monarchs, world leaders, and sell-out audiences, and attracts numerous awards in recognition of his outstanding contribution to classical music.

Apart from an unsurpassed musical pedigree and a playing technique par excellence, much of his popularity is due to his charisma and close rapport with his audiences. The fact that he has retained much of his Belfast accent, with no pretension to develop a more acceptable professional one, also endears him closely to his hometown audiences.

Galway grew up in Carnalea Street, off York Street, in a typical working-class terraced house. Many of the street's residents displayed various levels of musical ability on a range of instruments – accordions, tin whistles, flutes and banjos among others – talents which, during periods of unemployment, could be profitably used for busking around the city centre. But it was his father, Jimbo (as he was known to his workmates), who was the biggest musical influence on young James.

Jimbo Galway was something of a non-conformist. His family described his job as that of a riveter, but according to his workmates he was a 'straightener' – a semi-skilled trade which involved leveling out bumps in shell plates – and a job which, unlike that of a riveter, did not ensure constant employment. At other times he worked as a Heater Boy or Catch Boy for one of the riveters.

Jimbo was always popular with his colleagues, and was a reliable source of fun – he could be depended upon to indulge in the most unpredictable actions at work, without inhibition. Often on a Friday afternoon, as he headed along the Queens Road towards the cross-Lagan ferry (which left the gantries jetty carrying York Street-bound workers) he would cause embarrassment to his companions by abruptly stopping in his tracks and taking up position on the pavement among the throng of homeward bound workmen. He would toss his cap to the ground and burst into song, ignoring the startled stares of the passing crowd. After an impromptu ten-minute performance, he would recover his cap and the money his singing had attracted. With a cheery wave to his audience, he continued his journey home, his pocket much heavier than it had been an hour earlier. Although, like a lot of the workers, Jimbo was known to have a 'drough' (a drink) every so often, he never kept the collections for himself. At the first opportunity he would donate the entire amount to the nearest charitable cause.

His behaviour at home was no less uninhibited. On one occasion he was having a weekly wash in the tin bath in front of the kitchen fire – a standard routine in most two-up, two-down households as they were without proper bathrooms – when two female neighbours, who were passing by the unscreened window, stopped in their tracks and stood to watch him. When Galway became aware of their presence, he jumped out of the bath and, still naked, rushed to the front door and out into the street. The women screamed and, flustered, ran away. He pursued them along the street, completely naked, until his wife, who was beside herself with laughter, persuaded him to return to the house.

Jimbo played the accordion in a small dance band, which helped to augment his low shipyard wages but he also played the flute. He was devoted to classical music, in particular Mozart, and played in the Apprentice Boys' Flute Band, where he taught most of the new members. His wife, Ethel, was a competent piano player who, with her accordion-playing husband, was much in demand for local functions. One local resident remarked that there was so much music in Carnalea Street that it was like living in 'a musical pressure-cooker.'

Coming from such a household, it is perhaps not surprising that James Galway Jr sought a career in music. But, despite his fame, he remained close to his family, and to the father that had inspired him.

In the late 1970s, Jimbo became seriously ill so his son flew back to Belfast to visit him in the City Hospital. At the time, a small visiting choir was in the ward singing hymns. Galway, with his flute, joined in. He then launched into the 'Carnival of Venice' followed by variations. It is reported that his father, although sedated, was 'bursting with pride' to be in the presence of his famous son who had achieved so much. It was their last time together. A doctor had arranged to bring the patient by ambulance to a major Galway concert in Belfast a few weeks later. But, the day prior to the performance, Jimbo Galway died. The Belfast concert next evening became an unofficial requiem for a father to whom Galway was very close, and to whom he owed so much. Galway played Vivaldi's

'Four Seasons', arranged for the flute, with a passion that he later admitted he has never experienced before or since.

Today, despite his huge commercial success and the plaudits heaped upon him by his peers and audiences, Galway has remained remarkably modest, never forgetting his working-class Belfast roots. 'When I read a newspaper headline or article acclaiming me as the "greatest flautist of a generation", I know that, deep down I'm still wee Jimmy Galway from Carnalea Street'.

It is that self-effacing assessment of his extraordinary talents and honest tribute to his humble roots that endears him to audiences far beyond his native Belfast.

## George Best

Bob Bishop worked as a riveter in the Victoria Yard (or the 'Wee Yard' as we all called it). Like most workers in that trade he was almost deaf due to the incessant ear-shattering noises from riveting and nearby caulking machines. When in conversation, even in a quiet room, he wrapped his arm around a companion's shoulder and, from a distance of only inches, shouted into the listener's ear. It was an embarrassing and uncomfortable experience until one became used to it, and often it was necessary to respond in the same way.

Bob was relatively unremarkable and anonymous as a shipyard riveter, but far beyond the Harland & Wolff slipways, he was much better known for his role as a football talent scout. Over the years, Bob Bishop's name has turned up in numerous books, on the internet and on TV (on one occasion he even made an appearance on *This is Your Life*).

Bishop was an unpaid voluntary club leader at the Boyland Youth Club in Lomond Avenue, Holywood Road – a club where I spent nine years as a member. The building was shared with Lomond Primary School who used the premises during the day, while the club took place in the evenings. The facilities were minimal, but what the club lacked in modern amenities was compensated for by highly enthusiastic members and dedicated leaders.

Bob's main focus was sport, particularly football, and over the years he had nurtured many young players in the club's successful, trophy-winning team, Lomond Star. From the Boyland team a significant number of players progressed later into careers in full-time football either locally or in England – players including Jacky Scott, Tommy Lucas, Eric McMordie, Jimmy Nicholson and Isaac Magill.

Bishop had a natural instinct for recognising latent football talent in young people and the ability to encourage and develop it. He also had the unnerving ability to use barbed humour to put down those who did not meet his standards. At one time I had ambitions to play as goalkeeper in the club team. Bob kindly offered me a three-week trial period with Lomond Star. The results were disastrous for the club and my self-esteem. In the first two games, eight goals were scored against our team, an all-time record. Bob was always outspoken and one evening before the last match, I overheard him in the clubroom, in his loud voice, tell other boys, 'When Tommy's in goals, if a cartful of hay came near him, he wouldn't even catch a handful!' I took this unsolicited opinion very seriously. The same evening I made a voluntary exit from the team – before I was pushed!

On another occasion another team member was the butt of his wry wit – 'William is a very promising centre-forward. He's been promising to score for the last six weeks!' Even Matt Gordon, the club leader, did not escape Bob's comments. Mr Gordon had a receding hair line which attracted the observation, 'Poor Matt has more face to wash and less hair to comb every day.' Another time he seriously informed everyone that the high tower of St Patrick's Church, Newtownards Road, had been condemned. 'It was no longer safe to jump from the top of it,' he explained. A few of the boys actually conveyed this information to their parents!

When the Manchester United scout for Northern Ireland died, Bishop, due to his proven experience with up-and-coming young footballers, was deemed a natural replacement and was offered the position. Bishop made numerous trips around Northern Ireland to find new talent that could be referred to Manchester United.

Wearing his two hats as football scout and Boyland trainer, the Saturday matches were ideal opportunities to assess the talents displayed by the opposing teams in the Junior football league games. One weekend in 1961, when Lomond Star was playing against Cregagh Youth Club, a Belfast team, he was fascinated by the performance of one lad in particular. It was Bishop's first encounter with George Best, then fifteen years old. Even at that early age, Best's football skills in fieldwork, including dribbling and ball control with either foot, were phenomenal.

Bishop invited Best to share his weekend training retreat at Helen's Bay with the Boyland team. The results confirmed Bob's earlier assessment of the Cregagh Club's teenage player. He dispatched an urgent telegram to Matt Busby, Manchester United's manager. It was to the point and, with the passing of time, has become known as a classic understatement of fact and brevity – 'I think I have found you a genius.'

On Bishop's recommendation, George Best was given a trial with Manchester and was soon signed up for the team. In 1963, still only seventeen years old, he made his debut as a professional footballer against West Bromwich Albion. Over the course of his career, Best played as winger for Manchester United and the Northern Ireland national team. In 1968 he won the European Cup with United, and was named the European Footballer of the Year and the Football Writers' Association Footballer of the Year. He is described by the Irish Football Association, the national team's governing body, as the 'greatest player to ever pull on the green shirt of Northern Ireland'.

Almost everyone knows the rest of George Best's story. Early success with Manchester United, and his outstanding football skills and youthful good looks, made him a popular favourite with the fans on and off the pitch. At one time he was nicknamed the Fifth Beatle. Fame and recognition also brought him wealth and the trappings of wealth – cars, nightclubs, boutiques and numerous girlfriends. This lifestyle also exposed him to a world in which alcohol was an important element. It was an extravagant lifestyle of spending, drinking and womanising, and he became dogged by alcoholism and controversy.

Best's behaviour became more erratic. An increasing reputation for letting people down and a failure to appear at public events caused some loss of popularity and sympathy. On 8 August 1988, Bob Bishop and Sir Matt Busby stood together, possibly for the last time, at the Best Testimonial Match at Windsor Park, Belfast. (Best, displaying some of his old form, scored twice.) One can only speculate at what thoughts or conversation the two men shared as they contemplated the decline of their flawed football genius.

On 25 November 2005, George Best died. His death was attributed to lung infection and multiple-organ failure. The funeral, on 2 December, was one of the largest such events to take place in Northern Ireland. It was broadcast by British and Sky TV and seen by millions across the world. The cortège procession route from the family home at Cregagh to Stormont was lined with thousands and the packed memorial service in the Great Hall was relayed to twenty-five thousand mourners assembled in the grounds. It was an extraordinary tribute, akin to a state funeral, for a Belfast footballer from a working-class housing estate.

Best had been proudly held in great affection by most of his own countrymen, and by football fans everywhere. His career was a remarkable achievement for a Belfast teenager whose only previous football experience had been playing in Junior League against schools and youth clubs. It was also a tribute to Bob Bishop's outstanding skills as a trainer and talent spotter. He spared no effort in encouraging his young protégé's career in professional football on the national scene.

Sadly, another of Bishop's promising discoveries did not have the opportunity to progress beyond his native Belfast. On 21 July 1972 – Bloody Friday as it became known – the IRA exploded over 20 car bombs across the city, killing 9 people and injuring 130 others. A car bomb placed at Oxford Street Bus Station killed six people, one of whom was fifteen-year-old William Crothers, an employee in the bus station's parcels office. Crothers had been a long-time friend of Bishop, and a gifted footballer – a promising talent whose life was cut tragically short.

Bishop remained a powerful influence on the footballing youth of Belfast throughout his lifetime, probably surpassing any other character in the field of sport. But what is most incredible is that during this time, when he had the ears of men like Matt Busby or George Best, he was still carrying on his day job as a riveter in the Harland & Wolff shipyard!

# THE PHILANTHROPIST

Aristotle Onassis the Greek shipping tycoon – probably better known to a wider world when, in 1968, he became Jacqueline Kennedy's second husband – was the largest shareholder in Harland & Wolff. He made an attempt in the early 1970s to gain overall ownership but his proposal was rejected by the British government. But despite his disappointment at being denied control of the prestigious shipbuilding industry and the consequent advantages for his own group of companies, he was richly compensated in other ways.

He had placed orders for two super tankers, *Olympic Banner* and *Olympic Brilliance*, which were delivered in 1972 and 1973. They were fixed-price contracts. The overrun costs were considerable but Onassis refused to make any significant contribution to offset the real costs to the shipyard. The eventual losses to the Yard were at least a million pounds. These were only part of other loss-making contracts which were inexorably edging the shipyard towards insolvency. But Onassis, although a shareholder, was not unhappy. He had obtained two modern ships at a knock-down price!

To Queen's Island workers, he was their benefactor: his ships had provided much-needed jobs. Harland & Wolff's accountants may not have been happy, but Onassis was jubilant – as was the shipyard's Welders' Football Club and Social Club, then situated in Queen Street, Belfast. As a generous gesture Onassis had donated five thousand pounds to the new club in appreciation for the men's work on his tankers.

It is possible that a few workers were familiar with the saying 'Beware of Greeks bearing gifts!' but it certainly must have been a phrase that the shipyard Board of Directors could relate to. They were too aware of the true source of the Welders' Club donation.

Two years later, on 20 March 1975, the company minutes of a board meeting briefly recorded 'with regret' the death of Aristotle Onassis.

# THE TRAMS

Until the 1950s Belfast had an extensive network of tramcars which ran along most of the city's arterial roads, with a range of other public transport vehicles. For most passengers, a tram was just another means of getting from one place to another. Not if you worked in the shipyard! A Queens Road tram journey was an experience.

Every afternoon at quitting time, a line of trams – up to about twenty at a time – would stretch along the road outside the Main Offices and Deep Water terminus, awaiting the yard's army of homeward-bound workmen. Belfast Corporation, which operated the service, always put on their oldest vehicles (possibly with justification) – the blue-and-white Chamberlains, or the older Standard Reds which had been converted from horse trams many years earlier. The modern, streamlined versions, the blue-and-white McCreary's (the City Hall had a tradition of naming their trams after the managers who ordered them) were reserved for the rest of the system.

At that time until the late 1950s, few cars were on the road, and all sorts of methods of transport, including hundreds of bicycles, could be seen emerging from the shipyard at quitting time. But the most widely used form of transport was the tram. Thousands of workmen poured from the various workshops, slipways and fitting-out jetties to converge on the waiting trams on the Queens Road. In the melee, most of the pushing, heaving mass would head for the leading vehicle so that they could get away first. Officially the Chamberlains could only carry sixty-eight passengers, but by the time the tram moved off, there would be at least eighty aboard and another six or so standing on the external rear fender. A packed Tokyo train had nothing on a Belfast shipyard tram! The process was repeated until the Queens Road was finally clear of workers.

When the older red trams were used and mixed in with the others, the situation was even more dramatic and frightening. These old trams were open-ended. Workmen stood on the rear fender, grabbing the nearest handhold, internal or external. Other workers also climbed on the fender and, with no grip available, clung on to the nearest coat or shoulder for safety. One slip and there would be a body under the path of the following tram. But the workers appeared oblivious to the dangers. The trams would move off carrying their passengers – inside and outside.

The biggest problem, for the conductors at least, was how to collect the fares. It was highly unlikely that conductors ever received the majority of the fares due. Some would move optimistically among the standing passengers packed into the aisles, extending a hand for the fares. Shipyard tram travellers, who were notoriously friendly, responded, but not with cash – conductors collected numerous handshakes, but no money! It was an even more futile task to collect fares from the men hanging on the exterior of the tram. Most of the time he received more handshakes or was told, 'Catch yourself on, auld hand. Can't you see I can't get my hand in my pocket? Do you want me to fall off and get kilt?' It was a futile exercise and many conductors did not even try.

For the many passengers that regularly used the trams an unforgettable part of the journey was the smell – dozens of workmen, still in their overalls and crushed together in the tight confines, carried with them the distinctive odours of their trades as well as their own personal odour. Painters, joiners, fitters and many others permeated the air with smells of paint, sawdust, engine oil and other strong, unidentified working substances. On a wet day, clothing in the process of drying out also contributed to the potpourri. An additional contributor to the atmosphere was the cigarette smoke. All trams displayed the official warnings: 'Smoking is prohibited in the lower deck' and 'Passengers are not allowed to ride on the platform or staircase'. The notices were cheerfully ignored and few conductors tried to enforce them. Occasionally a respite from the choking air was provided by the pipe smokers puffing out clouds of War Horse or a Gallaher's-blend tobacco, which masked some of the more offensive odours. It was always a relief when the tram reached Castle Junction in High Street and passengers alighted for other destinations. After the smog of a shipyard tram, the clean, crisp air, even on a cold winter's day, was invigorating.

Apart from the conditions inside, trams were noisy, swaying vehicles, trundling along on hard suspension, emitting their characteristic loud grinding sounds on the tracks when traction was momentarily lost, or when the tram came to an incline. The trams were uncomfortable, but they were not without excitement.

John Currie, an electrician who worked on the aircraft carrier, HMS *Centaur*, recalls one incident on his tram. He had boarded early and managed to obtain a seat downstairs at the rear. Five minutes after starting off, the tram came to a sudden halt. Immediately a warning shout rang out: 'Bulkies! Bulkies!'. Two Harbour Policemen had stopped the tram. One climbed to the top deck while his companion entered the lower. A periodic search for stolen property (or 'pruck' as it was known in the shipyards) was about to begin. The policeman pushed his way, with difficulty, through the men in the packed lower aisle, scanning all around for suspicious parcels or behaviour. But as usual all the workers were the epitome of innocence – smoking, dozing or chatting. Currie in his rear seat was less relaxed. A tin of red lead paint had suddenly appeared at his feet. As he pondered this, another item appeared – a bathroom tap. That was followed by a succession of other items – pieces of wood, hammers, red candles and other shipyard materials. They had been pushed under all the seats from the front of the tram until, by the last seat, they could be moved no further. Currie's feet were surrounded by the stolen items. He grew alarmed as the policeman approached. He knew he was in serious trouble. How could he explain all the Harlands property at his feet? The Harbour constable took in the situation and asked, 'Don't you think you are a bit greedy, mister, hoping to get all that pruck out of the yard? Some of you guys think you can get away with murder. You must think we're blind.' Currie started to explain what had happened, but before he had got too far, the other suddenly changed his tone. 'Forget about it,' he said, 'I'm only joking. You're not the first one to be caught like that. It's those thieving buggers in the front seats who are shifting stolen property. But take my advice: you may not be so lucky next time – always find yourself a different seat.' The policeman withdrew, taking the articles with him. It was the last time Currie occupied a rear seat no matter how packed the tram. A similar situation with a less understanding policeman could be disastrous.

Regular crews operated the trams and the passengers were on friendly terms with many of them. One particularly popular conductor was nicknamed 'Fiddler' Moore. He carried a violin in the cab and, in his waiting tram, he passed the time by playing traditional and popular melodies. He also composed and performed songs (not always welcomed) about the actions of shipyard workers he knew. The good-natured banter of Moore and other members of the tram crews did much to alleviate some of the less pleasant aspects of travelling home.

Regrettably, despite a close rapport with some of the crews, there was always a practical joker who, thoughtlessly, would upset them. On some occasions when the conductor was outside the vehicle, a mischief maker would ring the bell which was the signal for the driver to move off. The tram would drive away, accompanied by loud cheers from some of the passengers, leaving the hapless conductor still on the pavement. A tram arriving at High Street without a conductor required a plausible explanation for the waiting inspector.

Another regular jape was to untie the trolley rope at the rear of the tram. When released, the trolley arm flew up in the air, disconnecting it from the overhead power line, and the tram slowly ground to a halt. It was an action which caused much annoyance to everyone as it took time for the conductor to reposition the connection. In the meantime a queue of other trams would build up behind causing more frustration and anger.

Despite the overloaded trams, with workers clinging on to every available handgrip on the outside – actions which would not be permitted in today's health and safety climate – miraculously there appears to be little evidence of any serious accidents occurring. But many accidents did happen to cyclists whose tyres became trapped in the tram tracks and who were thrown off their bicycles into the path of nearby vehicles. Deaths from these and other accidents were not uncommon on the Queens Road and at Station Street, which itself became a dangerous bottleneck for shipyard traffic of all varieties during rush-hour periods.

In 1939 the Belfast Corporation decided to eliminate the tram system, upgrading instead to trolleybuses (electric buses that draw electricity from overhead wires). However these never served on the Queens Road route – possibly the installation and running costs were a factor, as the tramway system operated mainly during the morning and afternoon peak periods. From 1953, the city tramcar services were gradually phased out and replaced with omnibuses, including on the shipyard route, and on Saturday 27 February 1954 tram services in Belfast ceased completely.

A ceremonial closing of the system was marked by twelve Chamberlain trams arriving on the Queen's Road from the Ardoyne depot. Souvenir tickets at 6d (3p) were issued for the occasion. At 11.30 a.m., the procession of trams, packed with enthusiasts, departed from the Main Offices stop for the last time. It passed over the old route – Queen's Bridge, High Street and along the Shankill Road to Ardoyne. A week later, without further ceremony, the trams were moved to the former tram depot on Mountpottinger Road to be broken up for scrap (though several of the cars which operated on the Queen's Island route were saved and are now on permanent exhibition at the Ulster Folk and Transport Museum).

It was the end of an era for the shipyard tramway service, which had opened in 1908 when Harlands was going into a major expansion period with orders for the *Titanic*-class liners. Throughout recessions and two world wars, the tramway system had served the Queen's Island community consistently with a reliable, cheap service. It might also be argued that in a unique way, despite its shortcomings, it made a vital contribution to Harland & Wolff becoming the world's leading shipbuilder.

# THE 7.10 A.M. WORKMEN'S TRAIN DISASTER

All shipyards have a history of accidents, often fatal, involving their workers. However the workers are usually philosophical about the hazards of the conditions in which they work and accept that these are par for the course. But serious incidents involving shipyard men outside the confines of Queen's Island always have a deeper impact on emotions and memories. One such incident occurred just two hundred yards outside the shipyard gates on 10 January 1945.

It was a typical winter morning, with poor visibility compounded by the thick fog which shrouded east Belfast. A workers' train, packed mainly with shipyard men, had left Bangor station at 7.10 a.m. After the train had passed Victoria Park Halt, where two hundred men had disembarked, the driver was alerted by a danger signal. He stopped the train between Victoria Park and the next stop, Fraser Street Halt (today's *Titanic* Halt), and awaited signals clearance. Following well behind was the Holywood railmotor special – a lightweight railcar that only operated between Holywood and Belfast.

The railmotor, comprising a leading heavy control bogie, two passenger carriages and a rear locomotive, had left Holywood at 7.40 a.m. A danger signal at Sydenham Station halted the train for several minutes. Then, following the instructions set out in company regulations, it proceeded cautiously to Victoria Park Halt where it dropped off some passengers. The Holywood train continued through the fog towards its next stop, the Fraser Street Halt (which was just past Dee Street Bridge). A few minutes later there was a violent impact when the leading bogie of the motor train struck the rear of the Bangor train which was stationary opposite the Oval Football Grounds, still observing the Ballymacarret danger warning signal from earlier. On impact the motor train's heavy front coach mounted the rear of the other train, ploughing through it and continuing into the next carriage, demolishing both of them into matchwood. In those two carriages 23 people were killed instantly and 24 injured, some seriously.

Workmen at the front of the Bangor train who had escaped injury scrambled out and began pulling away twisted metal and doors to release the trapped passengers. Bonfires of wreckage were lit along both sides of the wrecked carriages to help rescuers to see as visibility was so bad, and the injured were placed beside them. Empty buses returning from the shipyard and the aircraft factory of Short & Harland parked along the short section of the partially-built new Sydenham Bypass (work on this had ceased upon the outbreak of war). Their headlights and the bonfires illuminated the scene as doctors and nurses worked feverishly to save the more seriously injured. There were examples of remarkable bravery. One nurse, at great personal danger and despite repeated warnings, crawled into the mangled wreckage to help an injured man trapped under a heavy beam, and managed to release him.

The guard of the Bangor train, James Hewitt, although injured, reported later, 'When I realised what had occurred, I ran back along the track waving my red lamp and put down a number of detonators as a signal to the next Bangor train which was then almost due. In the darkness and with the line blocked it would have been a simple matter for it to pile up on the wreckage.' Hewitt's quick reaction undoubtedly prevented another tragedy and an even greater loss of life.

It was a grim sight that daylight brought to the eyes of spectators. Scattered around the tangled wreckage of the two trains were the passengers' personal belongings – lunchboxes, clothing and other items – relics of a tragedy that had occurred on a routine journey that hundreds had made many times previously.

The most amazing escape was that of Isaac McQuillan, driver of the Holywood train. Although his control cabin was wrecked as it ploughed into the rear of the Bangor train, he suffered only minor injury. Some were more fortunate than others – Bangor man, Sam Aiken, was a crane driver in the shipyard Engine Works. That morning, being late, he missed the 7.10 a.m. train. His normal seat was always in the rear carriage. He survived. Ernest Stitt always travelled in the same carriage on the 7.10. a.m. train, along with his brother, Robert. On the morning of the crash, he left the train at Victoria Halt. Robert, who was a labourer in the shipyard, was killed. By a tragic coincidence, two adjoining houses in Southwell Road, Bangor, lost family members – Stephen Lennon, a boilermaker's helper in the Victoria Engine Works, and Thomas Crosby, employed in the East Twin power station. Another tragic death was that of J. Hawthorne, of Conlig, a father of eight who worked in the Joiners' Shop.

The accident attracted widespread expressions of sympathy from many quarters – from Stormont, churches, councils and others, including the Lord Mayor of Dublin. A few days after the accident, the Mayor of Bangor had already received donations totalling over a thousand pounds.

Although the Second World War was nearing its end and the heavy losses of life in the Belfast Blitz were still fresh in people's minds, a public long-accustomed to news of tragic events was deeply shocked that a routine, early morning train journey could end in such horrific loss of life and injury.

The later public enquiry concluded that part of the blame for the collision rested with the driver of the Holywood train for travelling at excessive speed in poor visibility. The company, the Belfast and County Down Railway (BCDR) was also strongly criticised for lax operating procedures that resulted in drivers passing danger signals.

The accident was a defining event in the BCDR's history – it was a relatively small independent railway system operating within one county, with lines to Newcastle, Ardglass, Donaghadee and Bangor as well as various branch lines. It seldom enjoyed large profits. But during the Second World War, thanks to greatly increased military and civilian traffic, it built up a healthy Contingencies Reserve of one hundred thousand pounds which could be used to upgrade and re-equip the railway after the war. Unfortunately the January 1945 accident resulted in compensation payouts of eighty thousand pounds. Although the loss of capital to modernise was a major factor, growing competition from road transport and the anti-railway attitude of the Stormont government made the BCDR no longer viable as a public service. In 1950 most of the network closed down, ironically leaving only the Bangor line intact.

For the thousands of Islandmen who passed the scene of the accident in the days and weeks that followed, it was a poignant reminder that tragedy, when it does strike, is an unpredictable aspect of human existence.

# FRIDAY NIGHTS

Friday evening – end of week and pay day! After a long week's toil on the Queen's Island it was time to relax or celebrate. Thousands of workers poured out of the yard, thronging Station Street, Dee Street and the cross-Lagan ferry – in most cases they were homeward bound.

Many, still in their overalls, however, headed straight for their favourite pubs before they went home. For them it was tradition! The pubs themselves became an extension of the workplace they had just left. Many of the discussions or topics of banter (apart from football) involved their jobs in the Yard that week – the latest news about the Hats or gossip on fellow workers. In a 1960s BBC documentary, shipyard tradesman Alec McAvoy related how plumbers, getting together, would dip their fingers in their pints and sketch pipe layouts on a table to demonstrate how problems were resolved that day. Tommy Patton, a riveter and later Lord Mayor of Belfast, described how before the workmen arrived at the pubs on the Newtownards Road, the barmen had dozens of pints lined up on the counter to save time – these were then topped up to serve the thirsty shipyard men.

The image of tired workmen enjoying a quiet drink and socialising with their friends after a hard week's work is a cosy one, but for many families the reality was vastly different. Too many of the workers who headed for the pub were doing so at the price of heartbreak and hardship for their families. Their wives would not see them until the pubs had closed which, in those days, was at 10 p.m. They would already have spent much of their pay, including the amount intended for buying food and running the household. Many families, for weeks on end, would receive nothing at all.

At times, a man's wife had to resort to borrowing from relatives or taking items to a pawnshop on the Saturday morning to obtain some much-needed cash. But often there was no fallback at all and children would have to survive on crusts and anything else that could be cheaply obtained. As most women had a strong sense of independence and pride, very few neighbours would be aware of their dire plight.

A regular practice to ensure that essential household pay survived intact was for a wife to meet her husband outside the pub and relieve him of the money before he disappeared inside. A woman standing at a street corner near a pub, with a pram and children at her heel, perhaps in the depths of winter, hoping to grab the husband and the money before the barman got it was a common sight. It was a humiliating routine for a woman and a distressing experience for the children, as they watched their father walk away and leave them, not to be seen again until he arrived home late, drunk, and often in an aggressive mood.

This, sadly, was the culture of the times and until the early 1960s the male of a household had the dominant role – but even given the times, the behaviour of many men was feckless, selfish and beyond comprehension. But women can be resourceful in difficult situations, particularly when children are suffering. On occasion, if a man arrived home drunk as usual and with no pay to hand in, there was some recourse. As he lay in an alcoholic stupor his wife would raid his pockets and remove most of what cash was left. Once sober, he assumed he had spent more in the pub than intended, or had lost the remianing money.

On the Newtownards Road, where many shipyard men lived, there was a surfeit of public houses. Between the

Bridge End and the Holywood Arches, a distance of just under a mile, there were around twenty pubs. And close to each pub was a bookmaker's premises which, on the Saturday, along with the pubs, siphoned of much of a worker's remaining money. But not all bar owners were heartless businessmen – the owner of Murray's pub on the Mountpottinger Road had a conscience. He earned the nickname of Holy Joe due to his refusal to supply excess drink to customers known to have young families. The proliferation of pubs and social clubs in east Belfast was, to a degree, replicated in other working-class areas of the city (though their absence on the more affluent roads of Belfast would justify an interesting study by a sociologist).

Today, only one public house of the original twenty remains on the Newtownards Road. Thanks to the closure of Harlands, thousands of thirsty Islandmen no longer pour out of the shipyard into the streets on a Friday evening, in search of alcohol and gossip.

# A QUESTION OF BONUS

Apart from a normal weekly wage, most shipyard workers qualified for a bonus.

Some tradesmen were assessed on the amount of work they completed and received a 'piece-rate' bonus based on the amount of work they did. So for a riveter, say, a 'time and motion' inspector stayed with the worker and assessed how many rivets were installed during a certain period of time. A rate fixer would then inspect the quality of rivets installed and count them. These reports would be collated and used to work out how much of a bonus the riveter would receive with his basic pay at the end of the week. If his production eased up, this would be reflected in a lower bonus. As a result, workers with piece-rate bonuses needed little incentive to work harder, and most of those trades had the hardest working employees on the Queen's Island.

For the rest of the workers, all jobs under construction across the Queen's Island complex, however large or small, had a number which corresponded to the ship for which the part was destined. The time spent on a completed job would be recorded by a charge hand or Gaffer. The information would be later used to calculate a Completion Bonus payment when the ship was completed and handed over to the owners. It was a bonus many workers received, including apprentices, but there was no real pressure to work harder as it wouldn't result in a greater bonus.

Not all workers divulged their extra earnings to their wives on payday. And very often the secrecy sparked domestic quarrels. In a period now long gone, the neighbourhoods of Belfast terraced houses were close communities. Neighbours would often visit each other's homes to discuss the latest gossip, usually under the pretext of borrowing a cup of sugar or tea. It was an effective grapevine system used for updates on the latest happenings, local or elsewhere. Like all gossip, these conversations were often an inadvertent source of trouble.

Freddie Parker and Louis Morrison worked alongside each other in the Plumbers' Shop. They were also neighbours in the same street on the Oldpark Road. One day they were delighted to find in their pay slips an extra twelve pounds, the bonus for their work on a completed oil tanker. Louis, as usual, handed to his wife the complete wages envelope. Freddie, less open, gave his wife the usual Friday wage – the bonus, not known about, was his personal property, or so he reasoned. 'What the eye doesn't see, the heart doesn't grieve for,' was his philosophy.

It was a tactic that worked well until the following Tuesday evening when he was confronted by his furious wife. 'What happened your twelve-pound bonus?' she demanded. Taken aback, Freddie could only stammer 'What bonus?'

'You know right well what I'm talking about. Your completion bonus. I had Madge Morrison in today and she told me that the plumbers had received twelve pounds back bonus. I haven't seen yours yet.'

Freddie was cornered but, as always, he was quick on the uptake. 'Oh, that! You'll never believe this – it's so downright unfair. I couldn't join that scheme because I'm not in the Orange Order. That's why I miss all the bonuses.'

'Are you sure?' asked his wife, 'Madge never told me Louis was an Orangeman.'

'Ach,' replied Freddie, 'Sure, I thought everybody knew. Doesn't he go out every Twelfth of July with his sash in his pocket? He's very shy about it.' Freddie relaxed as his wife dropped the subject, apparently satisfied, although still muttering under her breath about discrimination in the shipyard. He had had a narrow escape but was saved by his wits – until the next day. It was a cold wet evening when he arrived home, looking forward to his usual piping hot plate of stew and placing his feet in front of the coal fire. As he opened the door, he received a sudden blow to the face. His wife had struck him with the coal shovel! As he staggered to his feet he managed to gasp out, 'What's that for?'

'That's for telling me a pack of lies,' she said. ' I spoke to Madge this morning and she said her Louis was never in the Orange Order. He was only in the Buffs. What do you say to that news?'

'You're absolutely right,' replied Freddie. 'I mixed up the two organisations. I really meant the Buffs.'

'You're still at it,' she shouted. 'Why can't you tell the simple truth for once? You kept my money and probably blew it at the bookies. And let this be a lesson to you, never do that again.' And she delivered another blow to the side of his head with the shovel. 'Another thing, you put that money in my hand next Friday, or else.' The 'or else' bit worried Freddie.

With blood streaming from cuts in the head, he made a final plea, 'I don't know why you never believe me. But to prove I'm on the level I'll get the money to you somehow. I'll have a word with Sir Frederick Rebbeck, the Chairman. Me and him are very friendly. I meet him regular down in the Anchor Bar in Ann Street. He owes me a good turn, and I'm sure he'll sort it out.'

The next day at work Freddie approached Louis. Before he had a chance to speak, Louis said, 'I notice you've got stitches in your head and a split lip. Have you had an accident?'

'Sure, and I wasn't eating chips, either. It was caused by that bloody wife of yours,' said Freddie. 'Could you not train her to keep a civil tongue in her head? She's got me into a hell of trouble at home. She's been blabbing away about those bonuses. Why didn't you just keep the money like everybody else and neither would have been any wiser?'

'Sure I couldn't do that,' said his friend. 'My Madge and me have a very open understanding with each other.'

'Well, if I can't give my wife twelve pounds on Friday I'll have a very open head and you'll visit me in the City Hospital. To save my bacon as well as well as my health, there's only one thing can be done. You will have to lend me the money and I'll pay you back the next time a good winner comes up at the bookies.'

'You must be joking,' said Louis, in shock. 'Why should I lend you money I'll probably never see paid back?'

'You have no choice,' said Freddie. 'After all it was entirely your fault I'm in this pickle. You might be my friend but I have to be honest with you, it's spineless, henpecked people like yourself that causes problems in other peoples' marriages! Now, what about that twelve quid you owe me?!'

# THE WORKERS?

Some employers today like to relate an anecdote which they claim as original and applicable to their own staff situation – a story which, unknown to them, actually had its origin in the Queen's Island many years earlier.

Sir Frederick Rebbeck, the Chairman, was conducting a potential customer on a tour around the extensive shipyard complex. The shipping owner, impressed by what he had seen, commented, 'Sir Frederick, with a workforce here of thousands, you must have a huge weekly wages bill. How many people work here?'

Rebbeck replied, 'As far as I'm led to believe, about half of them!'

# GOODBYE TO THE SHIPYARDS

As a young apprentice, my introduction to the coalface of shipbuilding had had a strong impact on me. The range and scale of shipbuilding activities at Queen's Island provided a fascinating and intimidating experience which was enhanced further by the knowledge that the yard's products and reputation would extend to oceans and ports far removed from my native Belfast. I was now part of that process. My family had had long associations with Harland & Wolff, dating back over several generations to the *Titanic*. Someday, I reflected, my own sons and, probably, grandsons would carry on the family tradition of working in the shipyard in a dangerous, poorly paid industry. But eight years after starting my apprenticeship, I broke that strong family tradition when I abandoned the Queen's Island and the joiner's skills I had learnt.

I was still working in the Joiners' Shop where very little had changed. Andy Carville and I were still great friends, each absorbed in our hobbies and daily meetings in the toilet block but I was growing restless. The break came when I saw an advertisement in the *Bangor Spectator* for a position as a TV engineer with Sloan's electrical business in Market Street, Bangor. At the time I was earning eleven pounds a week as a shipyard joiner and the change would mean a hefty drop in pay to seven pounds but, with my wife working and her encouragement, I made a successful application. In September 1957, I packed up my joinery tools for the last time and said goodbye to Queen's Island. Frankie Anderson accepted my resignation with some shock – few ever left the shipyard unless they were laid off.

In the decade that followed I had many careers and held many positions, including that of television engineer, senior civilian technician at RAF Aldergrove, owner of a TV and radio business, and engineer with the Civil Aviation Authority (CAA). Throughout this time, I remained friends with Andy Carville who, along with hundreds of other workers, had been laid off from the shipyard. Most would never work at their trades again – Harlands' terminal decline was under way.

Andy, a fine joiner, could only obtain a job as a Belfast bus driver, while our old friend Billy Lonsdale became a handyman in a city furniture store. But old interests kept us in touch. For three years Carville and I played together in the Lord Beaconsfield Accordion Band, but with the onset of the Troubles in 1968, the band wound down. Andy only lasted a short time on the buses before he was forced to retire on health grounds. Sadly, he never worked again and died a few years ago.

I was fortunate to have left Harlands before the mass payoffs took place. I spent twenty-eight years with the CAA as Air Traffic Engineer before my retirement in 1993, and from 1985 I had a second job with our family company, Bargain Books – a chain of bookshops that specialised in remaindered book titles. There I found that the old skills of woodworking learned in the Joiners' Shop could still come in useful as there were always jobs to be done – putting up partitions, building counters, making repairs and so on.

The shipyard days now seem so long ago but I still retain fond affection for the place and the many friends I made there. It is sad to see how such a famous shipbuilder has virtually disappeared. The area once dominated by gantries, cavernous workshops and slipways is now populated by hotels, offices, apartment complexes and tourist attractions

– buildings that will perhaps never inspire the same pride and affection that many of us felt for the Belfast shipyard. But I hope that the likes of the Titanic Belfast museum, with its exhibits and archive records, will ensure that the legacy of the world's greatest shipbuilders is kept alive. And that the Main Offices, the Thompson Dock and the Pump House (all original structures) will survive to inspire many, and remind visitors of the world-famous industry that once thrived there.

# THE SHIPS

# RMS *TITANIC*
# – FACT AND FICTION

RMS *Titanic* was one of three enormous passenger vessels commissioned in 1907 by the White Star Line, a major British shipping company. William Pirrie, Harlands' Chairman, had convinced Bruce Ismay, Chairman and Managing Director of the White Star Line, to order three liners which would surpass in size and luxury any operated by the line's main transatlantic rival, the Cunard Line.

RMS *Olympic*, at 45,324 tons, was completed in 1911; RMS *Titanic*, at 46,328 tons, was completed in 1912; and HM *Britannic*, at 48,158 tons, was completed and requisitioned in 1914 as a hospital ship for the Admiralty. The enormous liners were universally acclaimed as superb examples of British enterprise and innovation in marine technology. They represented opulence and luxury sea travel on an unprecedented scale.

The ships understandably piqued the interest of the popular media. In January 1912, the *Belfast News Letter* referenced the new safety measures on board *Titanic* (namely the powerful, electronically magnetised watertight doors), declaring that Harlands were 'practically making the vessel unsinkable'. However, the 'unsinkable' claim was not one endorsed by the Belfast builders. Thomas Andrews, Harland & Wolff's chief designer, refuted the claim and recorded his objection: 'The press is calling these ships unsinkable and Ismay's leading the chorus. It's just not true.' But the unfortunate description would return later to haunt all involved with the *Titanic*.

On 12 April 1912, *Titanic* left Southampton on its maiden

voyage to New York via the North Atlantic route. Two days later it grazed an iceberg 329 miles off Newfoundland and sustained damage on its starboard bow, just under the waterline. A series of watertight compartments, designed to prevent internal flooding in the bows sections, were overrun by the rising water level. As the forward lower decks flooded, the bows were forced under. Eventually, with the weight of the internal flooding and loss of buoyancy, *Titanic* was dragged beneath the waves. There were insufficient lifeboats (there were only sixteen on board) to cater for all passengers and as a result, over 1500 people, including Thomas Andrews, died in the tragedy.

Pirrie was on his yacht recuperating from a near-fatal illness when, on 20 April, six days after the ship's sinking, he received the devastating news. His immediate reaction was of shock and disbelief – how could a modern, 46,000-ton ship suffer such calamitous consequences? 'Find out what happened to that ship!' he wrote in a telegram to Edward Wilding, chief naval architect at Queen's Island, Belfast. It was a sentiment that has echoed down the decades – despite major public inquiries in Britain and the USA, the debate and speculation surrounding the famous sinking continues unabated.

Two major public inquiries were held after the disaster, but both Harlands and the White Star Line were cleared of negligence. This was fortuitous as a verdict of culpability and the resultant insurance compensation payouts would have bankrupted both companies. But disquiet about the verdicts soon began to circulate. Among the dissenting voices was *Titanic*'s senior surviving officer, Charles Lightoller, who had had a miraculous escape from the sinking ship. As Second Officer on the ship he was a prime witness at both inquests, but he claimed later that the investigations had been flawed, that the inquiries were really whitewash exercises that protected the reputations of the two companies as well as that of the White Star Line's owner, American financier J.P. Morgan. It was also significant that Lord Mersey of Toxteth, who presided over the British inquiry, was a personal friend of Lord Pirrie.

It is perhaps not surprising, then, that a multitude of myths and rumours about the circumstances of the calamity began to circulate – that Captain Smith shot himself as the ship went down; ill-disciplined officers shot male passengers who tried to enter the lifeboats; third-class passengers were locked below decks, unable to escape; and, most bizarre of all, the story of a large Newfoundland dog that jumped into a lifeboat and steered it from the sinking ship until its barking alerted the attention of the rescue ship *Carpathia*!

Conspiracy theories also began to emerge. One theory was that, in an attempt to test the strength of British shipping before the outbreak of the First World War, the *Titanic* had been attacked by a German U-boat prowling in the North Atlantic. One academic's alternative theory was that *Titanic* had struck not an iceberg but an ice field which, being low in the water, would be difficult to detect until too late. But perhaps the strangest and most entertaining theory emerged in the 1990s when Robin Gardiner wrote a series of books claiming that the *Titanic* had not sunk at all! That the disaster was an insurance scam executed by co-conspirators Harland & Wolff and the White Star Line and that it was actually the *Olympic* that had perished. The *Olympic* had, in 1911, suffered serious damage in a collision with naval ship HMS *Hawke* at Southampton and, as White Star was judged the guilty party in the accident, there would be no insurance compensation payout to underwrite the repairs. According to Gardiner, White Star and Harlands hastily and cheaply patched up the fatally damaged *Olympic* and switched it with the *Titanic*, planning to sink it in a controlled collision with another White Star ship, but that *Olympic* (posing as *Titanic*) missed the rendezvous with the collision ship and met an iceberg instead.

In more recent years Swiss writer Erich Von Däniken put forward an even less credible explanation. Däniken, an enthusiastic exponent of New Age topics and the existence of ancient astronauts, claims that he has strong scientific evidence to suggest that an underwater UFO fired two laser missiles at the *Titanic* and the attack was witnessed by Russian and Greek ships.

And it is not just conspiracy theories that have surrounded the *Titanic* disaster – claims of supernatural occurrences and premonitions are also prevalent. One lasting paranormal theory was that of 'The Mummy's Curse'. W.T. Stead, an influential, campaigning London journalist, was a passenger on the *Titanic*. During dinner on the evening of 14 April, he told the story of the mummy – a 1600 BC high priestess from the temple of Amon Ra, in ancient Egypt. Since the mummy's discovery, a series of calamities, including deaths, had followed those associated with it. Stead, not being superstitious, had bought the mummy from a shady London dealer, and announced to his fellow diners that he had clandestinely brought it on board the *Titanic*. He feared it might not be permitted on the ship and so had concealed it in a Renault automobile (a later scrutiny of *Titanic*'s cargo manifest confirmed that there was no mummy aboard but a Renault car was listed). Two hours after dinner *Titanic* struck the iceberg – coincidence?! – taking the priestess and many others to a watery grave. It is suspected that Stead's Mummy's Curse story was concocted as dinner table entertainment, but years later it still has credence among some *Titanic* enthusiasts.

On a less dramatic level, it has been reported that some passengers had premonitions and forebodings about the *Titanic* and its fate and cancelled their sailings to New York. It is alleged that there exist nineteen recorded premonitions. There have also been rumours that many of the crew recruited to sail with the liner refused to do so. Their fears were apparently based on a superstition about workmen who had lost their lives while the ship was being built.

There is a factual record of the reaction of Henry Wilde, former Chief Officer on the *Olympic*. He had been transferred to the *Titanic* at Captain Smith's request. When the crew assembled at Queen's Island he wrote a farewell letter to his sister – 'I still don't like this ship. I have a queer feeling about it.' A week later Wilde was dead, after playing a heroic part in evacuating the *Titanic*'s passengers.

Charles Lightoller admitted to no such trepidation and told fellow officers that he was content to have a position on such a wonderful ship. However he did express other misgivings. He and Sixth Officer, James Moody, had explored the routes from lower steerage (the third-class quarters) up to the upper lifeboat deck. He later recorded that they had had serious concerns that in a sudden emergency, due to the distances involved and the maze-like layout, third-class passengers would have little chance of escape. 'You could actually walk miles along the decks and passages covering different ground all the time. I was thoroughly familiar with pretty much every type of ship afloat, but it took me fourteen days before I could, with confidence, find my way from one part of the ship to another.' It was a prescient observation. It could also partly explain the disproportionate fatality rate of those in the lower decks – 25 per cent of steerage passengers survived, compared to 60 per cent of first-class. Though some social commentators cite the disparity in survival rates as evidence of a wealth–class bias in the evacuation priority – the rich first; women and children next; third-class passengers last.

The *Titanic* story, and the many conspiracy theories that surround it, has not only spawned countless books – one academic claims that the literature on the ill-fated liner exceeds anything written about Jesus Christ or the American Civil War – but films, plays and even an opera have been produced, exploiting an insatiable public appetite for the subject. (As the respected, and sadly missed, Belfast minister, the Reverend Derrick Bingham, once stated, the two most famous ships in the world are the *Titanic* and Noah's Ark!) For the longest time, however, these were produced without the support or approval of Harland & Wolff.

In the 1950s, Ulsterman William McQuitty, a producer with Rank Films, proposed a film on the disaster. He had witnessed the *Titanic* launch from the gantries slipway when he was just six years old and it had left an indelible mark on him. But when Sir Frederick Rebbeck, Harlands' Managing Director, was informed about the project, he was vehemently opposed – 'Bill,' he said, 'I don't mind it being done in fifty years time, but not now.' So, when McQuitty requested use of the official footage of the 1912 launch, Rebbeck refused – 'Certainly not, and I won't have any film people in my yard.' Undaunted, McQuitty went on to make *A Night to Remember*, based on Walter Lord's bestselling book of the same name.

Harlands rebuff of McQuitty was not unique. It was repeated many times in the future. Tom McCluskie worked for Harland & Wolff for over thirty years. An ex-apprentice, he had progressed through the office system in the main yard, eventually becoming the Archive and Administration Manager at Harland & Wolff, responsible for the company's archive of technical documentation and historic material. There was a massive amount of archive material in the Main Office – much going back to the earliest days of shipbuilding in Belfast – including the records relating to RMS *Titanic*, and McCluskie would often receive requests from around the world for information on the ship but Harlands' policy was clear – the company would rather forget that the disaster had ever happened. McCluskie had to respond with a standard statement – 'The company is unable to assist you with the information you requested.'

However the interest in *Titanic* continued – Ulster has two active *Titanic* societies, and other groups have flourished across the world, in places as far-flung as Florida, Adelaide and Ontario. McCluskie was made very much aware of the potential value of publicity for Belfast and Harland & Wolff in particular. Eventually he obtained permission from his superior to let him respond to the more serious requests for information, and in the mid-1990s, technical drawings were released to James Cameron, who was then making his major film, *Titanic*. McCluskie would later be seconded to the filmmaker as technical consultant.

The success of the blockbuster film *Titanic*, released in 1997, triggered an unprecedented renewed interest in the *Titanic* legend and McCluskie, aware of the worldwide interest in the tragedy and hunger for new information or souvenirs, launched the Maritime Heritage Collection. The marketing of *Titanic* replica material and linked merchandise was a huge commercial success, particularly in the USA and prestigious distributors, including TV companies, showed serious interest. The enterprise earned the shipyard much-needed profit and publicity, but Chief Executive Per Nielsen and Harlands' management (under Fred Olsen) claimed the Maritime Heritage Collection was making the company look like a museum rather than a shipyard, and it was shut down.

In recent years, this policy has changed drastically. In 2012, the centenary of *Titanic*'s sinking was marked by a series of commemorative events, including the grand opening of the new *Titanic* Belfast building on Queens Road, and Olsen cruise lines even operated a '*Titanic* Mini Cruise' which included stops at Liverpool, Southampton – and Belfast!

The appeal and fascination of the *Titanic* legend is timeless, and in the past few decades various entrepreneurs have made proposals to raise the sunken liner – even Boxcar Willie, the popular country singer and *Titanic* enthusiast, had plans to form a consortium and raise funds to recover and restore the ship. But the most significant results have come from those who have explored the wreck's debris on the ocean bed.

In 1985 Dr Robert Ballard, an experienced marine biologist and scientist working for the US Navy, used his advanced deep-sea robot craft, *Argos*, to search for the ship, and on 1 September 1985 *Argos*' remote cameras captured images of the *Titanic* – the first time the ship had been seen since 1912 – and Ballard made a significant discovery. The 1912 public inquiry had concluded that the *Titanic* had sunk in one piece, but the ship was actually in two separate sections – the badly-damaged stern was two thousand feet away from the bow, which was deeply embedded in silt, but otherwise fairly intact. In 1986 Ballard returned to the wreck site and his successful inspection and photographs made international headlines. His discoveries sparked off serious scientific interest in the ship, and prompted several subsequent expeditions to the site.

One expedition found a third section of the ship

separated from the others – the double bottom keel area. It would become a crucial element in constructing the *Titanic*'s last moments – did it sink intact and then break up, or did it come apart on the ocean surface? Conflicting evidence from surviving passengers and crew had testified to both scenarios.

In either case why did the *Titanic*, in unusually calm sea conditions, stay afloat for only two hours and forty minutes? In 1909, another Harlands-built liner – RMS *Republic*, of 15,000 tons – collided with the SS *Florida* off the US coast. A massive hole was ripped open in *Republic*'s starboard bow near amidships, causing extensive flooding into the ship's engine and boiler rooms. Yet it took the *Republic* thirty-six hours to sink, by which time its twelve hundred passengers (with only three fatalities) had been safely evacuated in a calm orderly operation to other ships. The same basic features present in the *Republic* were incorporated into *Titanic* and its sister ships.

Lady Louise Patten, the granddaughter of Charles Lightoller, offers one explanation. Using information that Lightoller had confided to his family, Patten, in 2011, wrote a book of fiction based on the disaster. According to Lightoller, Bruce Ismay had insisted the ship continue sailing after the impact, resulting in an accelerated rate of flooding. Had the ship remained stationary, it would have stayed afloat for several more hours, allowing more time for rescue ships to arrive, and perhaps more people would have been saved.

She also reveals that the impact had been caused by human error and was therefore avoidable – that when the iceberg was sighted straight ahead, an order was given to the helmsman to 'steer to port' (left) but Quartermaster Robert Hitchens had panicked and turned the helm in the wrong direction. (*Titanic*'s steering system still employed the older 'tiller orders' method whereby to turn a ship the helm had to be turned in the opposite direction to that intended, but Hitchens had been trained under 'rudder orders' and, whether by misunderstanding or in the panic of the moment, had swung *Titanic* to starboard, moving it closer to the iceberg.)

Other explanations pointed towards ineffective safety features on the ship. Andrews had built expansion joints into the *Titanic* and *Olympic* and fitted them to critical parts of the hull, parts that could be subject to the high levels of stress which a ship would encounter under rough sea conditions. These gave the long structure a safety margin of flexibility and bending without which the ship might break its back. The joints on the *Titanic* were fitted near the first funnel, just past the third funnel, and amidships. One expedition had given these expansion joints a detailed inspection and concluded that they were so crude and primitive that they would have been unable to protect the stressed hull as the bow's section listed under the weight of water in the flooded forward compartments. However, there is no consensus among other experts that failure of the expansion joints alone contributed to early sinking of the *Titanic*. What is agreed is that the ship fractured about amidships, near the third funnel, before or during its final plunge to the ocean bed.

Other experts expressed serious concerns about the quality of the steel used in *Titanic*'s construction, although Harlands had used the best steel available at the time. Analysis of the steel recovered from the wreck site revealed it had a tendency to become brittle at low temperatures and contained impurities that would reduce its structural strength and cause loss of ductility. Impurities were also found in the rivets – a combination of steel and wrought iron types were used in the bows, amidships and stern. These also indicated potential sources of hull failure.

Many argue that Harlands' global reputation for building safe ships using contemporary materials challenges the suggestion that inferior materials caused the *Titanic* disaster, but there have also been reports that the bureaucratic constraints placed upon Andrews by Bruce Ismay played their part.

Andrews was aware of the problems that building such large ships would create. *Titanic* and its sister ships would take shipbuilding design and technology into uncharted territory. As a result, he had specified 1¼-inch steel plating for the hull and crucial stress-bearing interiors, but was overruled by Ismay on grounds of extra costs and weight. Ismay defended his decision as the Board of Trade (BOT) requirement was only for 1-inch plating.

The limited number of lifeboats on board was another example of the BOT's outdated regulations (created in 1894). These specified that sixteen lifeboats would be sufficient for all ships exceeding 10,000 tons. Andrews and the general manager, Alexander Carlisle, had specified forty-eight lifeboats, but this request was also vetoed by Ismay – a cost-cutting interference which condemned hundreds of passengers to a freezing death in the mid-Atlantic.

In August 2005, an expedition sponsored by Lone Wolf Documentary and the History Channel carried out an extensive survey of the wreck site. Among the group was Roger Long, an expert on marine forensics, with years of experience on ship design and investigation of wrecks. A detailed inspection of *Titanic*'s three underwater sections and forensic analysis of a salvaged 20-ton hull section raised in 1988 provided clues, at last, to a possible explanation for the liner's ultimate tragedy – the appalling loss of life.

The popular perception of the ship's sinking, and one

endorsed by the public inquiries, was that progressive flooding of the forward compartments pulled the bows under the stern section, gradually up-ending to a steep angle before plunging under the surface in one piece. But Long, through evidence compiled from a computer reconstruction of the liner's final hours and metallurgical tests of the recovered wreckage, indicated that after the initial flooding in the bows, *Titanic* had settled in the water at a moderate forward list, no worse than would be encountered in a heavy sea. He theorised that there would have been no real indication of imminent danger to the passengers and crew, resulting in a reluctance to believe the ship was sinking and slow progress in filling the lifeboats. After all, a sojourn on a slowly sinking ship awaiting probable rescue was a more attractive option than descending down the sheer side of the *Titanic* in a swinging lifeboat, into the darkness of a hostile sea.

Long suggests that, just two hours after the initial flooding, while the liner was still at an unthreatening nine-degree list, catastrophe suddenly occurred. The ship began to fracture and bend, becoming 'hob backed' – as several survivors observed from their positions in the escaping lifeboats – and the front section, already partially flooded, broke away and sank. Water flooded into the exposed mid bowels of *Titanic* and its time afloat was cut short. The stern of the buckled ship, with its numerous internal compartments and air pockets, remained afloat for five more minutes before rising sharply in the air and, with its propeller shafts fully out of the water, partly rotated before plunging quickly below the surface. It would have been a horrific awakening from complacency for most of the passengers – any possible hope of rescue had gone.

Long's findings were sensational. He had questioned conventional wisdom about the sinking, and the world was incredulous. More significantly, he had surmised that the *Titanic* would not have broken up under normal stressing of its hull unless it was inherently flawed in design and construction. If it had not struck an iceberg, the primary cause of flooding, he believed it would have broken its back and sank in a voyage through heavy seas at a later time.

Long's theory placed the responsibility of the disaster squarely with Harlands – a position that attracted fierce opposition from *Titanic* historians. It was, however, a theory that found support from Tom McCuskie, the yard's archivist. In 2006, McCluskie, since retired, learned of Long's theory and, in a conversation with the expert, divulged significant information that he had been keeping to himself for a long time – that Harlands had implemented a deliberate cover-up on the *Titanic* once they realised they had, perhaps unwittingly, built a structurally flawed and unseaworthy vessel.

During his private study of archive design documents and Andrews' memos, McCluskie had learnt about Ismay's cost-cutting interventions and an investigation into the disaster by Edward Wilding, Harlands' chief naval architect.

Pirrie, on returning to Belfast, had ordered Wilding to carry out an internal Harland & Wolf investigation on the liner's loss. Wilding was briefed on the pattern of flooding and, with his knowledge of the ship's internal construction, was able to calculate that the area of hull damaged by the collision did not exceed 12 square feet. However, as the flooding was at high pressure, the ship was still destined to sink. He estimated that it would have remained afloat for around three to three-and-a-half hours – it sank in two hours, forty minutes. Wilding's investigation suggested that the *Titanic* had probably broken in half on the surface, prematurely reducing its survival time and the chances of survival for passengers awaiting rescue. This was devastating news for Pirrie. If the report was made public, it would destroy Queen's Island's integrity and reputation. It would reveal that the much-publicised liners were unsafe and unseaworthy.

The *Olympic* was recalled from service and both it and its sister ship, *Britannic* (which was still under construction) had major modifications carried out – double bottoms up to the water line; higher watertight forward compartments; and improved expansions joints were fitted. They were considerably stronger ships than *Titanic*, and *Britannic* had an additional expansion joint.

Wilding, meanwhile, was ordered to keep his report confidential and Pirrie instructed him to volunteer no unnecessary information on the *Titanic*'s design or construction at his public inquiry appearance. The public inquiries eventually declared that a 300-feet gash on the starboard bow was the primary cause of the liner's loss and apportioned blame for the disaster squarely to Captain Smith for sailing at excess speed after iceberg warnings had been received. Wilding's report was consigned to the yard's dusty archives.

When the report was finally disclosed over ninety years later, one feature of it threatened to undermine its validity and Wilding's credibility. He had estimated that the rupture in the bow was only 12 square feet – while experts through the years had estimated that this would have actually been 300 feet long. Who was correct? Previous expeditions to find the long gash had been unsuccessful, as the forward section of the ship was buried in 60 feet of silt. However, a more recent expedition, which employed advanced sonar-scanning equipment, penetrated the silt for the first time, revealing six narrow slits, each no wider than a human finger. The total area was about 12 square feet. Wilding, with his rudimentary slide-rule calculations, had accurately diagnosed the *Titanic*'s damage long before twenty-first century scientists with all their advanced technology had reached the same conclusion. Another widely accepted myth had been debunked – a remarkable, if belated, tribute to the knowledge of Queen's Island naval architects.

The people of Belfast are justifiably proud of their city's industrial heritage and the work produced at Queen's Island is a major source of this. So when the topic of the *Titanic* arises, the usual response is, 'It was all right when it left Belfast.' Today, however, other voices – formidable, scientific voices – are stating otherwise. Can they be ignored?

# REINA DEL PACIFICO

The *Reina Del Pacifico* was a magnificent example of Queen's Island engineering and opulence in passenger ship furnishing. Built in 1931, at 17,700 tons it was the largest and fastest motor liner of the period. With a striking all-white hull and orange painted funnels, the 'Queen of the Pacific' was the flag bearer of the Pacific Steam Navigation Company (PSNC). It was registered to carry 886 passengers and operated the Caribbean and South American route. It first came to the notice of the wider public on 9 November 1937 when the former British Prime Minster, Ramsay McDonald, died on it after suffering a heart attack.

Profitable and regular services were maintained until 1939 and the outbreak of the Second World War, when it was requisitioned as a troopship. Apart from two accidental fires and a later heavy attack by German aircraft when most of its luxurious interior was destroyed, it emerged from the war relatively unscathed. But wartime neglect and wear and tear had taken a toll on the once-pristine liner. *Reina Del Pacifico* returned to Belfast in 1946 for a major refit and conversion back to peacetime cruising.

On 2 September 1947, work completed, it left the shipyard for its sea trials. These were aborted almost immediately when, still in Belfast Lough, three of the four diesel engines overheated, and the partially crippled ship struggled back to the Yard for investigation and repairs.

Over 10 and 11 September, and for over thirty-three hours, the ship underwent successful trials through the Irish Sea and the Firth of Clyde. It was ready for the formal handover to the PSNC owners. But at 4.46 p.m., seven miles off the Copeland Islands, whilst doing thirty-three knots speed on its return voyage to Belfast, a port engine in the vast engine room exploded, showering burning fuel everywhere. A rapid series of explosions was triggered in the other three engines. The consequences were catastrophic.

Following the initial reports of the accident, several tugs and a Donaghadee lifeboat carrying doctors and medical supplies rushed to the anchored *Reina Del Pacifico*. The Royal Victoria and the Mater Hospitals were placed on emergency alert to receive the survivors, but in a serious and inexplicable delay, the first of these were only admitted eleven hours later.

A few days later the *Belfast Telegraph* reported,

> In an instant the engine room was a shambles. The lighting was extinguished, ladders and access platforms destroyed and the atmosphere thick with smoke. When rescuers entered the engine room they found fires breaking out and bodies everywhere. The appalling result was that twenty-eight people died instantly or from their injuries, and a further twenty-three were hurt. For three hours, Dr Ted Hamilton, in his first medical appointment, worked like a Trojan. Stripped to the waist, he was lowered into the darkness of the of the devastated engine room and, with the assistance of the First Officer, waded knee-deep in oil and twisted debris while striving to free men who were trapped. He then organised a first-aid service in the Second Class lounge, while stewards tore sheets and tablecloths into makeshift bandages. He is estimated to have bandaged nearly sixty men himself.

According to one eyewitness, the behaviour of Queen's Island management at the time was in stark contrast to the actions of Dr Hamilton. When rescue workers started to burn a hole in a bulkhead to obtain access to the injured in the engine room, they were stopped by a manager. He was more concerned about further damage to the ship than saving his men's lives. He was physically manhandled from the scene by angry workers and would probably have suffered a more serious fate had he resisted. His orders were ignored and a vital opening made to allow access to the injured men inside. Another example of Harlands' callousness came when they docked a half-day's pay from the injured men's pay packets.

It was a solemn and memorable occasion when the liner was eventually towed along Belfast Lough and docked at the Victoria Wharf. Only some blackening of the funnels hinted at the scale of the tragedy below decks. Hundreds of workmen vacated the workshops to gather silently at the dockside beside anxious relatives and journalists. Hardened shipyard men, too often familiar with violent death and injuries in the yard, stood with caps off and heads bowed as the *Reina Del Pacifico* was gently nudged against the wharf by the tugs. There was a palpable silence, with nearby machinery muted, as the bodies of fellow shipyard workers, draped in white sheets, were slowly carried down the gangway on stretchers to a long line of waiting vehicles. It was an overwhelming and poignant homecoming: an emotional scene for the grief-stricken relatives and workmates of the dead men and a stark contrast to the liner's proud departure on its routine sea trials only two days earlier.

What followed was a heartrending twenty-four hours for families and friends as they made the rounds of the hospitals and city mortuary to identify the victims. At one time five bodies remained unidentified, but by the weekend these too had been claimed.

Following the tragedy, letters of sympathy poured in from many parts of Britain. As a mark of condolence, the Belfast City Hall flag was flown at half-mast for several days.

Ulster Prime Minister, Sir Basil Brooke, sent a letter of sympathy on behalf of the government.

Among those killed was Leonard Brew, the Victoria Works manager in charge of the engines. Others had miraculous escapes. William Morrison was in the engine room at the time of the explosions and took the full force of them. He survived, despite suffering burns to 90 per cent of his body, and spent the following six years having regular hospital treatments. Leo Guilliano, a plumber working in the engine room, had a narrow escape. Ten minutes before the explosions he had left to wash his hands for the tea break. Another fortunate survivor was Tom Donnelly. He had left the engine room for a time and, on returning, was standing outside a door when the force of the explosions blew the heavy steel door towards him. He escaped serious injury. Many of the survivors suffered horrific injuries from burning oil, and required multiple operations for injuries to the face and body. Most ended up with permanent scars or disfigurements.

At the subsequent inquest the city coroner, H.P. Lowe, commented, 'The accident that happened on the *Reina Del Pacifico* ... seemed just impossible, but it happened.' A formal public inquiry held at Crumlin Road courthouse in June 1948 concluded that the primary cause of the first explosion was that one of the port engine's pistons had overheated and 'ignited an inflammable mixture present in the crank chamber of said engine'. The verdict about responsibility for the malfunctioning engine was inconclusive. The statutory legal procedure for establishing the cause of the tragedy had been satisfied and filed for posterity. Meanwhile twenty-eight families were still grieving the loss of loved ones and breadwinners. Their grief would not be so easily shelved and forgotten. An agreement between Harland & Wolff and the ship's owners, PSNC, resulted in both parties sharing the cost of compensation and repairs. It was an unusual arrangement as normally a ship's construction and seaworthiness were the builders' responsibility until it was formally handed over to the owners.

After repairs had been completed on the tragic *Reina Del Pacifico*, it went back into service again on the Caribbean and South American routes where it operated profitably for another eleven years. In 1958 the liner, which was one of the finest the Queen's Island had ever built and which had given many years sterling service in war and peace time, made its final voyage to Newport, Wales – the ship breakers yard.

# HMS *BELFAST*

On 30 September 1938, Neville Chamberlain, then British Prime Minister, returned home from Munich, brandishing the infamous non-aggression pact made with Adolf Hitler, and promising 'peace for our time'.

Only six months earlier, on St Patrick's Day, Chamberlain's wife Ann had uttered the traditional 'May God bless all who sail in her' at the launch of HMS *Belfast*, the Royal Navy's latest light cruiser named after the city of its birth. HMS *Belfast* had cost £2.1 million, and its contract had been won against strong tendering from five major British shipbuilders. It was 11,500 tons and had a main heavy armament of twelve 6-inch guns and other weaponry, including torpedoes. With a top speed of 32 knots (35 mph) it was the most heavily armed, technically advanced naval vessel of its type.

The crew accommodation onboard, however, was less impressive. One historian recorded that duty and working conditions aboard naval ships were little advanced since Nelson's time and HMS *Belfast* was no exception. In austere, cramped conditions, the 881-strong crew slept in densely packed hammocks, washed their own clothes in buckets and, allegedly, did their own cooking.

On 5 August 1939, one month before the outbreak of the Second World War, HMS *Belfast* was commissioned into active service and assigned to the 18th Cruiser Squadron, based in the bleak anchorage of Scotland's Scapa Flow as part of the naval blockade of German shipping. An early success for HMS *Belfast* was the interception and capture of three vessels – one of which was the German liner SS *Cap Norte* –

disguised as neutral Swedish ships that were in fact carrying war materials to Germany.

On 14 October 1939, a German U-boat penetrated the Scapa Flow defences and torpedoed and sank the HMS *Royal Oak*, a 33,000-ton battleship, causing the death of 883 seamen. *Belfast* survived that attack, but its good fortune run out on 21 November 1939 as it sailed from the Firth of Forth and became the first ship to fall victim to Germany's latest secret weapon – a magnetic mine. (Too late for the *Belfast*, a naval expert had successfully dismantled a captured mine on the east coast only two days earlier. Examination of the mine enabled countermeasures to be developed, namely the degaussing of ships' hulls, making them immune to the new weapon. Thousands of lives and numerous ships were saved by the action.)

At 10.58 hours *Belfast*'s ship's log recorded, 'Violent explosion felt on *Belfast*. Extensive damage.' At 13.14 hours, 'Prepared to abandon ship'. Twenty-one crew members were injured but, although disabled and without power, the *Belfast* stayed afloat. Under escort it was towed to a safe Scottish port for temporary repairs. The *Belfast* was taken to Davenport Naval Yard for major repairs but almost three years elapsed before the work was completed. HMS *Belfast* was finally re-commissioned for service in November 1942.

By then the ship was vastly modernised in armaments and mines protection. A vital addition was the revolutionary new ten-centimetre radar, which would play a pivotal role in the Battle of the Atlantic and also became essential to Bomber Command for precision bombing.

Back in the Scapa Flow, *Belfast* became the flagship of the 10th Cruiser Squadron whose role in the Northern Patrol was to protect the Arctic convoys carrying war materials to Murmansk in Russia. In 1942 alone, 6,714 tanks,

15,600 aircraft, 85,000 vehicles and millions of small arms and ammunition had been safely delivered by convoy to Archangel or Murmansk in northern Russia. But due to the twin hazards of enemy attacks and extreme weather conditions, the cost in lives and ships was high. Conditions at sea were appalling for Arctic patrols. Heavy waves constantly pounded the decks, producing large structures of ice and, since the additional top weight could endanger a ship, this all had to be scraped away. Crews would work on the heaving decks clinging to ropes with frostbitten fingers to avoid being swept overboard (seldom did anyone who fell overboard survive the freezing conditions). The crews, although seasoned seamen, were often seasick.

In late December 1943 HMS *Belfast* embarked on a new mission: it would play a key role in the Royal Navy's plan to trap and destroy the heavily-armed German battleship *Scharnhorst* (of 32,000 tons). *Scharnhorst* was the pride of the German fleet, and had already been responsible for the sinking of thousands of tons of Allied shipping, including the aircraft carrier HMS *Glorious* (also built in Belfast).

Having received intelligence that the German navy planned to attack the next Allied convoy headed from England to Russia, the Royal Navy arranged for two British convoys to make the journey to Murmansk, essentially acting as bait. At the same time, cruisers *Belfast*, *Norfolk* and *Sheffield* shadowed the convoys, while battleship *Duke of York*, the cruiser *Jamaica*, and four destroyers approached from the west. On 26 December, intelligence from the British code-breaking Station X at Bletchley Park, revealed that *Scharnhorst* had sailed with five destroyers on Christmas Day to attack the two convoys. It was only an hour away from its target when HMS *Belfast* and the two other cruisers arrived, taking *Scharnhorst* completely by surprise – the Battle of

North Cape had begun. The cruisers went on the attack: *Belfast* fired its six-inch shells over an eleven-mile distance and a shell from HMS *Norfolk* destroyed the *Scharnhorst*'s radar, but, as it retreated with the British ships in pursuit, *Scharnhorst* retaliated with its superior, faster-loading eleven-inch guns. A devastating barrage of Royal Navy fire virtually crippled the German warship.

HMS *Belfast* and the other cruisers moved in for the kill, unleashing torpedoes and deadly gunfire. *Scharnhorst* listed to starboard with fires burning furiously and by 7.45 p.m. the pride of Hitler's Kriegsmarine had slipped beneath the waves. Only thirty-six members of the crew survived while 1,932 men perished in the freezing waters of North Cape – such are the grim statistics of war.

After the sinking of the *Scharnhorst*, HMS *Belfast* resumed Arctic escort patrols. One unusual cargo, on a return voyage from Murmansk, was 19 tons of silver bullion which was safely delivered to Britain on New Year's Day, 1944. In March, *Belfast* took part in two vital operations – the escort of Convoy JW 58 (another Arctic convoy sent from Great Britain to the Soviet Union); and the Home Fleet attack on the German battleship *Tirpitz*, which was anchored in a Norwegian fjord. The enemy ship sustained devastating damage but remained afloat. Crippled, and no longer seaworthy, it was non-operational until the final months of the war when, on 12 November 1944, a squadron of RAF Avro Lancaster heavy bombers finally sank it.

On D-Day, 6 June 1944, HMS *Belfast* played a key role in the Normandy Landings. As the flagship, *Belfast* controlled the Gold Beach sector – which supported the British and Canadian troops' landings – and at 5.30 a.m. it initiated the first salvo of intense naval gunfire from the massive Allied fleet that had assembled. Under *Belfast*'s control was

HMS *Glasgow* on which ex-shipyard electrician, John Currie, served. Years later he recalled his never-to-be-forgotten experience of the landings – the endless exploding shells, the ear-splitting noise, the smoke and the alarming reverberations that rocked the cruiser on each salvo. As part of the greatest sea armada in history, the *Belfast* and other warships pounded the German shore fortifications relentlessly until the landings and an inland beachhead had been secured.

The *Belfast* was in continuous operation for five more weeks, then returned to Britain for a refit and new armaments prior to deployment against the Japanese in the Pacific. In the final few days of the war, HMS *Belfast*'s good fortune held out. Unbeknownst to the crew, it was spotted in the North Sea by a German U-boat but, thankfully, the captain decided not to fire. *Belfast* had been in his sights and torpedoes were ready to fire, but by then the German forces knew that the war was lost. The U-boat captain's decision not to sink the *Belfast* was a logical and humanitarian gesture that undoubtedly saved hundreds of British lives.

Before *Belfast* saw active service in the Pacific, the atomic bombs dropped on Hiroshima and Nagasaki – on 6 August and 9 August 1945 respectively – ended the war. Japan formally surrendered on 2 September 1945.

With hostilities ended, the cruiser's new role, along with other Allied shipping, was the evacuation and provision of help for the thousands of civilians who had been interned by the Japanese. Emaciated, sick and dying people were ferried from Shanghai to Hong Kong for treatment in British hospitals. The last mercy mission of *Belfast* was on New Year's Day, 1946.

Nine years after leaving its birthplace, HMS *Belfast* returned to the city and, from 20 October 1946, there were several days of civic and military celebrations, including a march past the City Hall, watched by thousands of proud, cheering citizens. In a ceremony at the docks, on the quarterdeck, gifts from the city were handed over – a magnificent silver ship's bell and crest that had been in safe custody during the war years. On 23 October 1946 HMS *Belfast* sailed from Belfast Lough for the last time.

During the 1950–52 Korean War, *Belfast* was back in action and, on occasion, came under heavy gunfire from shore batteries. Damage was never serious, although one man was killed and others injured.

After another extensive refit between 1956 and 1959, the *Belfast*'s main role was 'Showing the Flag' around the world and sea exercises – an activity most navies employ in the absence of hostilities. For a time its less dramatic role was as a reserve ship, and it was used as a floating barracks. It looked like the ship would not be in active service for very much longer.

Fortunately for *Belfast*, in 1968 the Imperial War Museum (IWM) expressed its interest in preserving relics of great ships that had defended Britain and other nations across the world. Initially the museum had its sights on preserving a six-inch turret from a ship, which would then represent a number of classes of cruiser. After museum staff visited the HMS *Gambia*, they discussed the possibility of preserving an entire cruiser. However, HMS *Gambia* had deteriorated too badly so attention shifted to HMS *Belfast*. A joint committee was established by the Ministry of Defence, the IWM and the National Maritime Museum to consider the feasibility of preserving the *Belfast*. The verdict was that the proposal was economic and practicable but, despite this, the government's Paymaster General decided against preservation and in early

1971 *Belfast* was 'reduced to disposal' – naval jargon for 'sell or scrap'.

This did not deter a team of private individuals who established an HMS *Belfast* Trust. The campaigning efforts of this group met success when, in July 1971, the Admiralty handed over the cruiser to the Trust. *Belfast* was towed up the English Channel from Portsmouth, via Tilbury, to its final resting berth in London on the Thames, where it was fitted out as a museum.

In 1977, the IWM sought permission to merge the Trust into the museum. Shirley Williams, then Secretary of State for Education and Science, assented, stating that, 'HMS *Belfast* is a unique demonstration of an important phase of our history and technology.' The IWM gained possession on 1 March 1978, almost forty years to the day since the *Belfast* was launched.

Today HMS *Belfast* is a popular London landmark near Tower Bridge. It attracts at least a quarter of a million visitors each year, and over seven million people have already visited the ship. A welcome gesture of appreciation of the ship's role in the Arctic convoys came in 2008 when Vladmir Putin, Russian Prime Minister, donated one million pounds for essential repairs on the cruiser's masts.

A tribute from Admiral Sir Frederick Farham, a former captain of the ship, is worth recording: 'I had the immense good fortune to command HMS *Belfast* ... in what were, I suppose, the most exciting two years of her long life [1942–44] spent largely in the Arctic. Her designers and builders had made her the fine ship she was and still is. The officers and men who served in her and were proud to do so, made her the efficient and happy ship that she was throughout her successive missions.'

Now Harland & Wolff has almost completely gone:

its memory destined to fade into the mists of time. But on the Thames in London, one of the most cosmopolitan and famous cities in the world, sits HMS *Belfast* – a major tourist attraction which keeps alive the name of Ulster's capital city and, possibly, the name of the once famous shipyard that built it.

# RMS *MAGDALENA*
# – A MAIDEN VOYAGE

Thirty-seven years after the sinking of the *Titanic* on its maiden voyage, another Belfast-built ship was lost on its first sailing. The Royal Mail refrigerated cargo liner, the *Magdalena*, of 17,547 tons, was completed and left Queen's Island in 1949 for entry into the South American service.

On 25 April, while en route to Argentina, and carrying over 350 passengers and 100 crew, RMS *Magdalena* ran aground off Rio de Janeiro. Other ships safely rescued all aboard. Tugs were brought to the scene to refloat the liner but, as the ship was firmly caught on the rocks, the attempt failed and, instead, the ship broke in two. In most cases a vessel with a broken back is beyond economic repair and the *Magdalena* was no different – eventually it was salvaged as scrap.

Its brief existence, which ended on the ignominious maiden voyage, was an operational and economic disaster for the shipping company, but thankfully there had been no loss of life. If there had been, the reputation of the company might have been more commercially damaged. An enquiry was held at the Royal Courts of Justice, London, and the verdict was that the incident had been the result of poor navigation, with insufficient attention being paid to compass errors. Its captain had his master's certificate suspended for two years.

Despite these findings, doubts were raised about whether the ship had been seaworthy when it left Harland & Wolff's shipyard. Why did the new vessel break in two when it was subject to the stresses of the recovery operation? The matter was raised in the British House of Commons where the Minister for Transport, Alfred Barnes, reassured Parliament that the *Magdalena*, from the laying of the keel plate to its final inspection certificate on 18 February 1949, had conformed at every stage of its construction to all the ministry's survey standards.

Bill Harkness, a Belfast man, was the refrigeration engineer aboard the *Magdalena* when it ran aground. Years later he asked local heritage group, Lagan Legacy, to assist him in locating other surviving crew members and they managed to find three other ex-seamen in Britain and Australia. In April 2006, under the title of 'Four Men in a Boat', Lagan Legacy coordinated and organised a reunion of the four former comrades. By all accounts it was an emotional occasion for those involved, and it's quite likely that Bill Harkness, mindful of his roots, would not have missed the opportunity to remind all present that the loss of *Magdalena* was entirely due to poor seamanship – and not to any structural flaw in the Belfast-built ship!

# JUAN PERON
# – THE JINXED SHIP

Those who work in the maritime industry have a strong tradition of superstition and the idea that some ships can be jinxed or cursed is a recurring and popular one throughout seafaring history and fiction. Should a ship be deemed cursed or jinxed, shipowners find it difficult to recruit crews – on occasions, men have refused to take up appointed positions in such ships, although it is a mercantile marine offence.

Harland & Wolff, as the world's most prolific shipbuilder, inevitably had its quota of alleged jinxed vessels – the most memorable of these being the *Juan Peron*, an Argentine whaling factory ship of 24,569 tons.

Juan Perón, the President of Argentina, had ambitions for his country to be the economic and commercial super power of South America. To that end, generous state subsidies were granted to companies that wished to expand and promote the nation's international prestige. When the Perón government offered a 30 per cent subsidy for the production of the largest whaling factory ship in the world, Norway, with its dominant whaling tradition, strenuously opposed its construction. The Norwegian government applied pressure on the British government to halt the building of the giant whaler in the UK but, as any embargo would have been illegal, Harland & Wolff were able to begin work on the commissioned ship.

The *Juan Peron* was launched in 1950. Eva Perón, wife of the Argentine President, had been scheduled to perform the launching ceremony but political agitation back home against the Perón regime prevented her from leaving the country. Miss Irene McClurg, a secretary in the Yard's main offices, stood in her place, but the VIP's enforced absence would, in hindsight, be construed by some as a harbinger of worse to come. (Indeed, Eva would lose her life to cancer a year later and Perón was eventually deposed in a military coup).

After its launch, the *Juan Peron* was berthed at No. 2 jetty in the Musgrave Channel for final fit out. Still coated in its slipway red lead, and easily the largest vessel moored in the channel, it cut an impressive presence as it towered over all the others. In fact, the enormous whaling vessel rode so high in the water – with the main deck 80 feet above the jetty – the customary single wooden gangway from ship to shore was not practical. Instead a steel platform, welded to the ship's hull, served as an intermediary stage for two wooden gangways. The upper gangway ran parallel to the ship's hull and onto the steel platform, from which, at a right angle, the lower gangway extended down to the quayside. Nine months after the launch, while the Peron was still undergoing fit out, these gangways would be the scene of a devastating shipyard tragedy.

On 31 January 1951, ten minutes before the yard's klaxon signalled the end of the working day, thousands of men at various locations across the shipyard, were already poised for the stampede towards the timekeeper's huts to hand in (or more often, throw in) their time boards. Workers on the ships were not permitted to descend the gangways until the sirens sounded and their managers (the Hats), who blocked access to the gangways until the sirens sounded, stood aside to let them pass. On the various ships across the Yard, hundreds of heaving, bunched bodies thronged the exit decks waiting for their Hat to step aside, but on the *Juan Peron* it was a different story.

Earlier that day, the manager on the whaling ship had

taken ill and left early for home (much to the delight of many workers aboard the ship!) so at stopping time, as the workers assembled on deck to leave the ship, there was no one to control the situation. Before the sirens had sounded, around a hundred men had been pushed relentlessly by the others behind, on to the upper gangway.

The gangway was not designed to support a stationary weight of so many men and, as they stood in place, two ominous cracks rang out in quick succession. Several workers exchanged joking comments that perhaps the gangway was going to collapse. Without further warning, and before the workmen had grasped the danger, the upper gangway fractured into two sections. The men had no time, or room, to escape. All the men were pitched into the semi-dark abyss, 80 feet below. Most of the bodies landed on the dockside fender moored between the ship and the jetty, or on the concrete quayside. A few of the terrified falling workers made attempts to grab a lifesaving handhold – a broken handrail, a severed electric cable, or an air hose. Other men still on deck had the terrifying experience of being propelled on to the shattered gangway and into the void below, by the thronging crowd behind, who were still unaware of the danger. Harrowing screams of the falling men were short-lived as, with sickening impact, they piled up on the fender and jetty – crushed, broken or smothered. The swaying broken gangway also propelled some men into the freezing water of the Musgrave Channel. The tragedy was compounded when a part of the heavy gangway broke loose and landed on the fender with its pile of dead, dying and injured. Under its human load the fender tilted precariously into the water and threatened to submerge everyone.

Workmen on the quayside reacted rapidly to the harrowing scene confronting them. The victims that could be reached, whether they were alive or dead, were carried off to more secure, comfortable positions and basic first aid was applied to give some relief to the injured. Willing hands bridged the perilous gap between the jetty and fender to rescue others from the sinking fender. In truth, there was little the rescuers could do to help the injured men before the emergency services arrived, except offer reassurance and encouragement to the traumatised survivors. In the darkness of a wintry evening, illuminated only by the normal weak temporary lighting, an almost surreal atmosphere pervaded the scene. The mood was heightened further by the painfully poignant sight of the fractured gangway swaying gently in the breeze, and caps and lunchboxes floating in the water.

The rescue attempts continued. There was an occasional shout, 'We need more hands. There's some poor buggers in the tide. If they're not got out, they'll drown or freeze to death if not already gone.' Elsewhere a cry of recognition would be heard. 'I know this one – good lad, with a young wife and two kids. He left for work this morning like us all, now she's a widow and doesn't yet know it. Hell's bells! Who is going to break that news when she's expecting him home as usual?' Among the dead was a youth, probably an apprentice, who was still in his early teens. The discovery tore at the hearts of the rescuers already emotionally devastated by their efforts. Their helplessness was compounded by conjecture that some bodies were still in the water, trapped under the ship. If so, it was probably too late to rescue them alive. The shipyard's Chief Diver was soon on the scene but further searches could not be carried out until *Juan Peron* had been moved to the centre of the channel to deeper water, and arc lights set up. In late evening, working under difficult conditions, the diver located another body.

One workman, Davy Crawford from Altcar Street,

Belfast, had a miraculous escape. As he plunged off the gangway, he reached out wildly. Against the odds, his downward fall was arrested when his fingers grasped a narrow steel plate seam 80 feet above the water. He hung there for five minutes with only his bleeding fingertips supporting his entire body weight, until his screams for help drew the attention of workers still safely on deck. A volunteer was suspended upside down over the ship's side, with workmates holding his legs. As he was lowered down the hull he managed to grab Crawford's arms in time and saved him from falling to certain death in the freezing water below. Both men were dragged carefully back to safety on deck. It was an extraordinarily brave initiative – a heart-stopping and terrifying rescue action for both workers. Later when Crawford was interviewed, he admitted that the thought of his disabled son, Paddy, had given him the strength to hold on so long.

Another lucky survivor was joiner Wilson Haire, the father of the shipyard joiner and famous playwright of the same name. He had been near the gangway queue but had returned to a cabin to collect his forgotten lunchbox.

When the ambulance crews arrived, No. 2 quayside resembled a battlefield. Bodies were strewn everywhere, and many of the injured already seemed beyond help. The overwhelming images of lifeless and horribly injured workmates in their torn and bloodstained overalls was so grotesque that many who witnessed the scene would have recurring nightmares for years afterwards. Eighteen workmen died in the tragedy and fifty-nine were badly injured – some never worked again.

Days after the disaster rumours circulated in the shipyard that the gangway had broken at the thirteenth step, though most treated the news as the sort of baseless superstition that often attaches itself to any tragedy. The tribunal inquiry into the accident concluded that one of the longitudinal runners supporting the steps was flawed. It had given way under the abnormal concentration and excessive weight of the workmen. As there existed no Board of Trade mandatory regulations on gangway construction, Harland & Wolff were absolved of negligence or responsibility. One interesting factor confirmed by the tribunal was that the gangway had indeed fractured at the thirteenth step.

By October 1951, *Juan Peron*'s fit out was completed and it was ready for delivery to the owners, Compania Argentina. A protracted payment dispute arose between the shipyard and the owners, and the whaler remained at Belfast well past the handover date. As a result of political and economic changes in Argentina the whaler company developed financial problems and *Juan Peron* was sold off to another whaling company, who renamed it *Cruz Del Sur*. The new owner's fortunes were no better – for a time the ship was impounded at a foreign port when the owners were accused of money laundering; and after eight years of operations in the Antarctic, not a single whale was caught or processed.

The jinx reputation grew when it was reported that a girl had been murdered on the ship and her body thrown overboard. It also acquired a reputation as a ship that was difficult to sell, though it did change owner several times. One report claims that when no longer relevant as a whaler, it was cut in two by a Japanese shipyard and converted into drilling platforms. In 2008, under its latest name of *Ismay* – a title with tragic *Titanic* connotations – it was being used as a floating warehouse off the Indian coast.

# SS *CANBERRA*
# – THE GREAT WHITE WHALE

Ship No. 1621 was launched from Harland & Wolff's East Yard on 16 March 1960 by Dame Pattie Menzies, wife of the Australian prime minister. Commissioned by the Peninsular and Oriental Steam Navigational Company (better known as P&O), the ship symbolised the company's commitment to building a new generation of the largest and most opulent passenger liners afloat. It was, as P&O declared in their promotions, 'The ship which shapes the future' – a confidence which, in time, would be amply vindicated. The ship would go on to exceed the owner's most optimistic predictions, shape the destiny of the builders and play a pivotal role in a crucial episode of British history.

P&O, formed in 1840, was the premier British shipping line, providing much of the essential communications and trade infrastructure that powered the expansion of the British Empire in the nineteenth century. Its passenger and freight services operated on routes via the Iberian Peninsula to the Orient and, due to the company's long association with the colonial mail ships, its passengers were also carried to Australia and New Zealand via the Mediterranean and the Suez Canal.

Over the years the company had expanded to become the foremost passenger and freight carrier in Britain – having absorbed many other smaller lines in the process. At its peak in the 1920s it owned almost five hundred ships (though it lost 185 ships during the Second World War). After India's independence in 1947, passenger traffic from there declined, but was fully compensated for by an influx of

British and European emigrants into Australia. The majority of the million new settlers had sailed on P&O liners as 'ten pound Poms' under the assisted passage plan established and operated by the Australian government to encourage British subjects to migrate there after the Second World War. The scheme ended in 1968, but fifteen new liners had been built post war to facilitate increasing emigration.

In the mid-1950s a further two super liners were commissioned to augment the existing passenger fleet to Australia and New Zealand. Speed, economy of operation, and passenger capacity in two classes were essential parameters in the design of the super ships. One, ordered by a P&O subsidiary, the Orient Line, was built by Vickers–Armstrongs Shipbuilders, Barrow-in-Furness. The other, ship No. 1621, was placed with Harland & Wolff.

The Orient Line had a tradition of giving their ships names beginning with the letter 'O' and, in keeping with the practice, the Vickers liner was named 'Oriana'. The name of the Belfast-built ship, however, remained undecided for six months (though one Harlands employee suggested the new ship should be called 'Orstralia'!). After discussions with the Australian prime minster, Sir Robert Menzies, permission was granted to call the ship *Canberra*, after the country's capital city.

Before the keel plate of the ship had been laid, its builders were confident that the completed liner would be unlike any other passenger ship in existence. It would represent a radical departure from traditional shipbuilding technology and design. Queen's Island would translate the conceptual drawings of P&O's architect into the template that would influence passenger liners' design in future decades. At 45,270 tons, *Canberra* would be P&O's largest-ever passenger ship.

When the partially built vessel slipped into the water it was a major social event. About three hundred invited VIPs and dignitaries, as well as ten thousand other spectators lined the Musgrave Channel Road to see the launch of the shipyard's greatest liner since the *Titanic*-class ships fifty years before. For the occasion the name *Canberra* – of aboriginal origin, meaning 'meeting place by the waters' – could not have been more appropriate.

By April 1961, final fit out had been completed. The ultra-streamlined hull had been partly inspired by the earlier 20,000-ton liner, *Southern Cross,* also built in Belfast. *Canberra* had a striking, elegant and flowing profile and, from every angle, its 820-foot-long white hull displayed classic curvilinear lines. The engine room and funnels were positioned near the stern, and the curved funnels, painted a distinctive yellow, were built side by side instead of in the traditional line-up.

A pioneering departure was to abolish lifeboat decks and, instead, to recess the lifeboats into bays nearer the waterline thereby freeing vital deck space and providing a clean unbroken superstructure. It was an innovation copied later by other shipbuilders. With fourteen decks, *Canberra* had capacity for 2,238 passengers and 960 crew. With the engine room and funnels placed aft, and the lifeboats 'nested' in the hull, spacious, open plan interiors for public use were created over more deck levels. The lavish facilities and décor were comparable to a five-star hotel, albeit with promenade decks and ornate staircases. Few commentators failed to report that the latest P&O liner was indeed a beautiful ship.

The ship wasn't just beautiful, however – every convention of shipbuilding had been challenged by Harlands in building *Canberra*. The work done for the engines and in propulsion technology was particularly innovative – a unique configuration of steam turbine and electric motors delivered a massive and unprecedented motive power of 42,500 horsepower to *Canberra*'s twin propeller shafts. It was the most powerful turbo-electric system ever installed in a passenger ship and in its Belfast Lough sea trials, it achieved a speed of 29.5 knots (33 mph) with a normal cruising speed of 27.5 knots (31 mph).

In a further break from tradition, the upperwork structure was constructed in welded aluminum, which served to reduce the overall structural weight and give better economy in operating costs. P&O would have preferred an all-welded ship, but the management at Queen's Island, under Sir Frederick Rebbeck's influence, preferred riveted shipbuilding – an outdated practice which caused higher costs and longer completion times.

When *Canberra* departed Belfast on 29 April 1961 it was a day of mixed emotions. Thousands of people thronged the Sydenham Bypass and the roads and beaches around Holywood and Bangor to catch a glimpse of the magnificent liner as it sailed along Belfast Lough. Lord Brookeborough (the Prime Minister of Northern Ireland), Denis Rebbeck and other dignitaries stayed aboard as far as Bangor before disembarking, and a sense of celebration filled the air.

But for the workforce that had built the ship, the overriding feeling was that of concern. For four years, construction of the *Canberra* had provided employment for hundreds of workers and craftsmen and, unless similar orders were received by the Queen's Island, there would be no future jobs for many of the fitting-out trades. The workers would have to seek jobs 'across the water' at other shipyards, or else face a life on the dole. Several men, more adventurous than others, did not wait for the work to dry up completely: they sailed to a new life in Australia with their families, some on the very ship they helped to build. One welder, Francis Bingham, obtained work in a shipyard in South Australia and, before he left Belfast, reflected, 'I regret leaving the old shipyard, for which you develop quite an affection over the years. I hope the place I am going to and the Gaffers are as good, for Harland & Wolff have been good employers. But I'm honoured and happy to sail to a new life on the *Canberra*. She is more than just a number to us shipyard men. She is a household name in every yard man's home in Belfast. Even the kids in the street know where the *Canberra* was built.'

Regrettably the fears of the Queen's Island workers were not groundless and *Canberra* was the last passenger ship ever built by Harlands. Further orders that might have been gained on the back of building the prestigious super liner did not materialise. Thousands of craftsmen never worked in the shipyard again. The other contracts obtained were for specialist vessels that required fewer workers and fewer fitting out tradesmen.

There was even grimmer news for the Harland & Wolff directors. Construction of the *Canberra* had been negotiated on a fixed-price contract with a rather tenuous agreement that P&O would cover any overrun costs. From the original estimate of £11.73 million, the final cost had soared to £17 million but, after prolonged negotiations, the ship's owners only agreed to an extra payment of £1.5 million. Historians agree that the unsustainable loss on *Canberra* was a knock-out blow for Queen's Island, one which, combined with future loss-making contracts, set the shipyard on a course from which it would not recover.

The fortunes of P&O, however, were vastly better. *Canberra*'s commercial operations commenced on 2 June 1961, with a three-month voyage from Southampton to Australia, New Zealand, Hawaii, USA and Canada, and the ship was fully booked in advance. In Melbourne the ship met with a tumultuous welcome. Among the welcoming party was Dame Pattie Menzies, who remained on board as the ship sailed on to Sydney. The publicity surrounding *Canberra*'s maiden voyage had been so great that when it sailed under Sydney Bridge, the city was brought to a standstill by enthusiastic sightseers. The *Sydney Morning Herald* reported, '*Canberra* has rightly been called a floating showcase of beauty and craftsmanship. We are justifiably proud of her – not only of her immense size, comfort and revolutionary design, but also of the role she is destined to play in making ocean travel faster and more interesting for her passengers.'

Despite engine problems during the voyage, the new addition to the P&O fleet had proved that the normal five-week voyage could be reduced by a week. During its early years in service – which were spent mainly on the Australian/New Zealand route – occasional technical hitches caused disruptions in the service, but these did not distract from the ship's popularity. Despite being a few knots slower than the *Oriana*, its main competitor within the P&O fleet, *Canberra* became the flagship of the company.

The 1960s were a lucrative trading period for passenger traffic but, by the end of the decade, social changes were taking a toll on traditional modes of travel. The end of assisted travel to Australia and New Zealand reduced the volume of emigrants but a more threatening challenge came from the growing popularity of air travel which could reduce five-week travel time to two days. Passenger liners would have to adapt to the new social climate to survive.

The obvious solution for P&O was to enter the cruise market so, using New York as a base, Caribbean Cruises was launched. Eleven cruises in all took place before the enterprise was judged a commercial failure. A decision was taken to scrap *Canberra* at the end of the 1973 cruising season, but before the ship breakers took possession, a sudden increase in the popularity of cruises occurred. P&O reacted quickly to the changing circumstances. *Canberra* was refitted to carry only 1,700 passengers in one-class accommodation and new amenities were installed. With a base at Southampton, short cruises operated in the summer, and longer ones in the winter months. The strategy brought immediate dividends and business boomed. It was a trend set to expand and continue until, in an unexpected turn of events, the *Canberra* assumed a more dramatic role in world events.

On 2 April 1982, the Falkland Islands in the South Atlantic were invaded and occupied by Argentine forces. The colony's only airport was controlled by the Argentines, so any counter invasion by Britain to regain the islands had to be a seaborne operation. It was a formidable military challenge to mount an offensive thousands of miles away from the UK, and only two British ships had the capacity to convey the essential troop numbers to the scene – the *Queen Elizabeth 2* (*QE2*) and the SS *Canberra*. The latter was mid-cruise in the Mediterranean when, on 3 April 1982, its captain was instructed to sail to Gibraltar. There it was revealed that *Canberra* had been requisitioned by the Ministry of Defence as a troopship. At Southampton, stripping out and major modifications were carried out, including the installation of three helicopter pads over the games area and swimming pool. Only a few days later, it departed Southampton loaded with vast quantities of equipment and ammunition, and 2,500 troops. Among these were the 40 and 42 Commando Royal Marines and a parachute regiment.

Along with the *QE2* and other naval ships, an impressive

flotilla of a task force was assembled to reach and relieve the occupied colony from the Argentine army which, by then, had reinforced their positions. On 21 May 1982, *Canberra* reached the war zone and entered San Carlos Bay to unload its troops. During the all-day operation the liner and other ships were under constant attack from Exocet missiles and low-lying enemy jet aircraft determined to sink the troopship which, with its immense size and brightly painted hull, was an unmistakable target. The aluminum superstructure caused much concern to all aboard – a direct hit and the ensuing fire would have been disastrous. To avoid enemy aircraft coming too close, *Canberra* launched its army blowpipe missiles in defence and, miraculously, escaped unscathed, despite being a sitting duck in the bay. Others were not so fortunate – HMS *Ardent* and HMS *Coventry* were sunk, as was *Sir Galahad*, which suffered heavy casualities.

With all *Canberra* troops and supplies landed in the face of ferocious attacks, a decision was made not to endanger the *QE2* – if that ship was sunk by the Argentines, the political repercussions and effect on morale in the UK would be significant. So after disembarking all its troops and equipment, *Canberra* rendezvoused with the *QE2* at South Georgia, well away from the battle zone, to take all of the latter's troops and stores. *Canberra* re-entered Carlos Bay to allow the troops to disembark and then, in its other role as a hospital ship, it collected the survivors from the attacks on the naval ships. The pivotal, and most dangerous, action in delivering the fighting task force to the Falklands had fallen to the *Canberra*. It was a vital contribution to the campaign to re-take the island, and all involved – the P&O crew and military personnel alike – performed heroically and professionally under fire.

On 14 June 1982, after stiff fighting across the islands

and with serious causalities on both sides, the Argentines surrendered. But *Canberra*'s role in the conflict was not yet over – the ship collected 4,167 enemy prisoners at Port Stanley for eventual repatriation to their own country. It was ironic that the ship which they had tried to sink only recently would return so many to the safety of their own country. It was a massive logistical operation – guarding, feeding and accommodating so many in a liner which had been converted to transport only half those numbers. On 19 June, escorted by an Argentine naval vessel, *Canberra* was safely piloted into a home port. A second repatriation of prisoners (of the overall 11,485 prisoners), followed later. The resident crew of the *Canberra* reportedly showed considerable courtesy and kindness towards the prisoners: after the ship had been cleared, P&O cleaners found numerous notes of thanks from prisoners expressing appreciation for the way they had been treated.

*Canberra* began its return to the UK on 25 June 1982 with 2,489 marines on board. After an absence of ninety-four days and sailing over twenty-five thousand miles, the 'Great White Whale' as it had been nicknamed, arrived in Britain on Sunday 11 July to an extraordinary welcome. As *Canberra* approached Southampton an armada of small ships surrounded it. On the quaysides an estimated thirty-five thousand people, in a sea of Union Flags and welcome banners, gave a tumultuous, jubilant homecoming to the returning troops. Elsewhere, away from the public frenzy and celebrations, others quietly grieved for the 255 people who never came back.

After the return from the Falklands and a sixty-three-day-long refit at Southampton to repair the ravages of war and to update the amenities, *Canberra* was ready to re-enter service. Thousands of well-wishers again lined the docks as the ship departed the fitting-out yard, small crafts packed the harbour, helicopters hovered overhead, and a military band performed a specially composed piece titled 'San Carlos'. There was extensive television coverage of the event. The celebrations demonstrated that SS *Canberra*, in its Falklands' role, had become a national icon which symbolised the UK's position of international prestige and authority.

Commercial service for SS *Canberra* resumed in September 1982 and a new itinerary was introduced to include seasonal cruises to Australia and New Zealand. They were an immediate sell out. The subsequent years brought prosperous trading to P&O. Much of the demand for the Great White Whale cruises can be credited to the 'Falklands' factor' and the high public profile it attracted. But, apart from its history, *Canberra* offered a wide range of cabin grades and recreational activities. It became the foremost cruise ship operating out of the UK – a British institution. Destinations were extended to cover Europe and the Scandinavian capitals and, for the first time, round-the-world cruises were made available to British passengers who otherwise could not have afforded them. It is on record that the many Belfast passengers on the liner were always keen to inform others that the luxury ship had been built in their city and that they or their relatives had been part of the actual workforce who built it.

In 1986, another major refit took place at the Lloyd Werft shipyard in Germany – Queen's Island no longer had the capacity or skills to compete for the contract. Modern furnishings and a new décor brought *Canberra* in line with its rivals in the fast-expanding cruise market.

But technology and time were edging up on the *Canberra* generation of cruise ships. In August 1989, Qantas Airways flew a Boeing 747 airliner non-stop from London to Sydney. It was an historic occasion, which the *Canberra*'s captain generously acknowledged, dispatching a message of congratulation to the Qantas pilot. And in the competitive cruise market, larger and more luxurious liners were being operated (though many of the new generation passenger and cruise ships incorporated design features pioneered in the *Canberra* over thirty years earlier).

But despite its advanced age, *Canberra* continued to trade profitably for P&O into the 1990s. One controversial passenger during this time was Lindi St Clair, the famous twentieth-century prostitute. Lindi had been involved in several sex and tax scandals when she was spotted on *Canberra*, and her time on the ship was equally controversial. Her request to the ship's bureau for permission to sunbathe topless on the decks was rejected, so she got revenge by borrowing an officer's hat and posing topless for photographs at the captain's table

A more dignified and memorable occasion for many was in 1994 when the British Legion chartered the ship to bring veterans to the Normandy beaches to commemorate the fiftieth anniversary of the D-Day landings. A Lancaster bomber flew over the *Canberra* and released a million poppies onto its crowded decks.

Across the world, the *Canberra* was held in very high esteem, epitomising much that is associated with ocean travel – adventure, romance and excitement. But, thanks to the actions of its crew and the loyal passengers it attracted, it also earned a reputation for being 'the friendly ship', no mean achievement in the often ruthless, competitive shipping market.

By 1997, age and costly maintenance costs of the engines made *Canberra* uneconomic to maintain as a cruise ship and after a final cruise to the Mediterranean, it was taken out of service on 30 September 1997. Another shipping line placed a bid for the ship, but P&O were adamant that it would never sail under another flag. It was eventually sold for £4 million to a ship breakers yard in India.

When Tom McCluskie, the resourceful Main Offices manager at Belfast, learned that the ship was to be scrapped, he persuaded P&O to donate the bridge-mounted shipbuilders' plaque to Harland & Wolff as a treasured memento. They agreed and the plaque was delivered to the shipyard – but to the wrong department and McCluskie never received it. Possibly, today, in someone's attic space or garage, the priceless *Canberra* relic languishes.

With a record thirty-six years of unbroken service, and having set new standards in ship design and luxury, ship No. 1621, which had its genesis in a Belfast shipyard in 1961, came to a honourable but predictable end in an Indian scrapyard. It was driven at speed on to the beach to aid breaking up, but the Queen's Island-built vessel was sturdier than expected and the task of demolishing the ship, estimated to take three months, took well over a year.

By 1998 *Canberra* had gone, but for the millions who had sailed on it, and for the craftsmen who had built this magnificent ship, the happy, proud memories will survive for years to come.

# ACKNOWLEDGEMENTS

Particular thanks go to David and Jilly Johnston who gave priceless encouragement and support to me while I wrote this book. A special mention should also go to my sons, Alan and Thomas, who introduced me to the baffling new world of computers and emails.

I am grateful to all the former Queen's Island workers who willingly shared their memories of times past and to Crawford Howard for the fascinating interview and for the kind permission to reproduce his iconic poem, 'The Diagonal Steam Trap'.

I would like to express my thanks to Dr Brian Walker of Friars Bush Press for republishing several Workman Clark promotional texts originally issued in the 1930s. Collected together in the book *Forgotten Shipbuilders of Belfast*, they were an invaluable source of information on Workman Clark.

I would also like to thank Alf McCreary for sowing the seeds and for inspiring myself and others to venture into the world of print.

Thanks also go to my publisher, Blackstaff Press – Patsy Horton, Managing Editor, and her staff. Particular appreciation is due to Michelle Griffin for her advice and for patiently guiding me through the consultation and editing processes of publishing.

And finally, I am very grateful to my long-suffering wife, May, for her patience over my neglect of numerous domestic chores, which were put aside to facilitate *Auld Hands*.